Handshakes not Handcuffs

Proposals for Co-operative Alternatives to the European Union

Edited by
Lionel Bell

The June Press

In Association with TEAM
The European Alliance of EU-Critical Movements

First published in 2002

by The June Press Ltd
in association with TEAM
(The European Alliance of EU-Critical Movements)

UK distributor
The June Press Ltd
PO Box 119
Totnes
Devon TQ9 7WA
Tel: 44+(0)1548 821402
Fax: 44+(0)1548 821574
EMail: info@junepress.com
Web: www.junepress.com

ISBN 0 - 9534697 -2-7

Cover design by Alice Leach

This book is printed on environmentally friendly paper
Printed in Great Britain by Kingfisher Print, Devon

Contents

Acknowledgements   V
Notes on Contributors   VII
Foreword   IX
Sir Oliver Wright
Introduction   XI
1   Europe of Many Circles: Constructing   1
     a Wider Europe. 1990
     Richard Body
2   A Europe of Nations. 1995   11
     European Research Group
3   The Breakdown of Europe. 1998   13
     Richard Body
4   Pour les états-généraux de   19
     la souveraineté nationale. 1998
     Alain Bournazel & Etienne Tarride
5   Europe - Démocracie ou Super-Etat. 2000   31
     Georges Berthu MEP
6   Associated, Not Absorbed.   41
     The Associated European Area: a constructive
     alternative to a single European state. 2000
     Bill Cash MP
7   Separate Ways. 2000   47
     Peter Shore
8   European Manifesto for a   53
     Charter of Sovereignties. 2000
9   Limits to EU Integration. 2001   57
     Lord Owen

CONTENTS

10   SOS Democracy's Thirteen Demands. 2001   61
11   The Manifesto of Czech Euro-realism. 2001   65
      Jan Zahradil & others
12   For a Europe of Democracies - Against   73
      the Europe of Nations. 2001
      Paul Ruppen
13   A Better Europe: 79
      Foreword from the Treaty of London. 2002
      Lionel Bell

Acknowledgements

The hard thinking that led to the proposals set out in this book has all been done by their originators and I must acknowledge the support I have received thereby. The selection and compression are mine and I am wholly responsible if these have resulted in any misrepresentation. I also wish particularly to acknowledge the contribution of Nigel Spearing in guiding me to material about the Council of Europe.

Lionel Bell

Notes on Contributors

Lionel Bell is the author of *The Throw That Failed*, a study of the first decision to seek accession of the UK to the EEC. He is Vice-Chairman of the Campaign for an Independent Britain and Secretary of the Anti-Maastricht Alliance.

Georges Berthu has been a member of the European Parliament since 1994 and is the author of several books on Europe, including *A chaque peuple sa monnaie*, which predicted the collapse of the euro, and *Traité de Nice: L'Europe sans repères*.

Sir Richard Body was a Conservative Member of Parliament from 1955 to 2001. He is Chairman of the Trustees of the Centre for European Studies and a member of the Editorial Board of *New European*. He has published a number of books on agricultural policy.

Alain Bournazel is Chairman of Action pour une confédération pan-européene and Secretary-General of Etats généraux de la souveraineté nationale. His other works include *La Souveraineté* and *Les Balkans - la guerre du Kosovo*.

Bill Cash MP has been a Conservative Member of Parliament since 1984. He served as Chairman of the Conservative Backbench Committee on European Affairs and is currently

Shadow Attorney-General. He has published a number of pamphlets on the EU and is Chairman of the European Foundation.

Lord Owen CH was a Labour Member of Parliament from 1966 to 1981, founded the Social Democratic Party in 1981 and led it from 1983 to 1990. He has held a number of Ministerial posts, including that of Foreign Secretary 1977-79, and from 1992 to 1995 served as EU peace negotiator in the former Yugoslavia.

Paul Ruppen is a political scientist, Chairman of the Swiss Forum for Direct Democracy and Editor of Europa-Magazin.

Lord Shore was a Labour Member of Parliament from 1964 to 1997, when he became a Life Peer until his death in 2001. He served as Secretary of State for Economic Affairs 1967-69 and then for Trade 1974-79. He has also published *Entitled To Know* and *Leading The Left.*

Etienne Tarride is an advocate at the Paris Bar and was formerly a Councillor in Paris. Committee member of Action pour une confédération pan-européene.

Sir Oliver Wright, GCMG was formerly H.M. Ambassador to the Federal Republic of Germany and to the United States of America.

Jan Zahradil is a Member of the Chamber of Deputies of the Parliament of the Czech Republic and Shadow Foreign Minister for the Civic Democratic Party (ODS).

Foreword

It has been said that after the destruction of the Twin Towers on September 11th the world in which we live has changed. And so, in a geostrategic sense, it has. Russia and the United States are now partners in fighting terrorism and reducing nuclear arsenals. China has rejoined the rest of the world in the World Trade Organisation. The 'rogue ideologies' - the phrase is Robert Conquest's - of the 20th century - nazism and communism - are - thanks to transatlantic solidarity and the commitment of the United States to democracy in Europe - on the scrap heap of history.

Changed, yes; but only up to a point. That other rogue ideology, Europeanism, embodied in the European Union, continues its mad destruction of the nation state, the sole and essential safeguard of peoples' liberties, along a route signposted by the Treaties of Maastricht, Amsterdam, Nice, and now Laeken. When will this monumental folly end?

Is it not significant that the 15 component states of the Soviet Union responded to the collapse of communism by recapturing their national identities? People want to govern themselves. Have the British people so soon forgotten that the three federations - Central African, Malaysian and West Indian - which they invented to facilitate withdrawal from Empire, all came apart at the seams almost as soon as the ink was dry on the treaties that created them. These rogue federations had common attributes; they were artificial political constructs, imposed from above and lacking democratic legitimacy. Just like the EU. When will we ever learn?

The merits of Lionel Bell's book are manifold. It reminds us that only the democratic nation state has the means to prevent the abuse of power, the main political source of misery in the world, by dismissing the government in office. To err is human, but only the nation state has the means to remedy past mistakes by installing an alternative government to do so. That the *acquis communautaire* should be held to be sacrosanct is the ultimate proof of the democratic illegitimacy of the Brussels institutions. The book not only makes a valuable contribution to the current debate by warning against repeating the mistakes of the past but also by assembling between its covers examples of viable and better alternatives.

Handshakes Not Handcuffs is a striking image of maximum co-operation with our continental friends but minimum integration with them. Such a vision works with the grain of our national sentiments, enhances democratic accountability and strengthens the transatlantic connection. The book is a wake-up call: let it not be said that our right to govern ourselves was taken from us while we slept.

Oliver Wright

Introduction

This book contains a variety of proposals for co-operative arrangements between European countries that have appeared in the last ten years as alternatives to the ongoing integration of the European Union. Most of them are summaries of relevant parts or excerpts from larger works that have been selected to demonstrate in a convenient form the breadth and depth of reasoned opposition to the EU in the shape in which it is now being constructed. Over this period it has steadily become more evident that not only has there been a failure to ask the peoples of Europe what sort of European co-operation they wanted but plans for a federal state are being imposed on them from on high. This has resulted in the European Union's institutions being perceived as remote from ordinary people, a view which has been accepted by at least some of their political leaders. The prospect of extensive enlargement, together with its use as a device for increasing federal power, has brought that perception into sharper focus. At the time of writing the proposals to be placed before the planned Constitutional Convention that have emerged from the Laeken Summit demonstrate continued determination to create a state called Europe by slotting in the final pieces. The patent lack of accountable democracy within the structure of the EU's institutions and national Parliaments cannot reasonably be brushed aside by feeble claims that scores of regional assemblies with puny powers will enable decisions to be made 'closer to the people'.

The originators of the proposals appearing in this book have grasped these points and set out to devise remedies that go some way, at least, to restore power to democratically controlled institutions. The book should thus be seen as a positive contribution to the debate on the future of the EU for which the European Council itself has asked. In essence the remedies are based on the principle of willing co-operation between democratic sovereign nations. Together they amount to a reasoned rebuttal of the Europhile claim that there is no alternative to the Union as it is today and is being planned. The proposals originate from a number of countries and display a wide range of approaches. They extend from those who see the solution in some modification of the fundamentals of the EU, *via* those who would retain some of its institutional features within a new set of arrangements, to those who would replace it entirely by a new and improved model. Some of the first group offer specific amendments to the Treaties on which the EU is founded, in some cases including prohibitions of particular expansionist activities to which those in charge of the EU might otherwise be attracted.

What is common to these proposals is that every one of them would serve the people of Europe better than the authoritarian command and control system that is the EU of today. They are not put forward here on the basis that an exclusive choice has to be made between them. They are not in competition with each other, even if their titles may apppear contradictory, but only with the EU. National governments - for it is they who will have to make the changes - could deploy any of them or any combination of them for different spheres of activity provided only that they are resolved to bring to an end their own participation in the federalist adventure of the EU and seek partnerships in other ways. Even the most limited proposals would require that degree of resolution and would leave countries in a position to adopt appropriate co-operative arrangements in matters in which they had recovered their liberty of action. All such arrangements could evolve and as some are seen to be more fruitful than others they might come to be used by new partners. There may be a role here for some modified institutions to promote, by assembling and disseminating information about them, the wider use of such constructive relationships as they are developed.

By no stretch of the imagination can these proposals be abused as anti-European. Indeed they are both pan-European and international. At the same time as they implicitly acknowledge nations' sovereign rights of withdrawal - even where they do not do so explicitly - they recognise that other member countries may wish to engage in some closer relationship, as long as it is not done in the expectation that all will follow in due course. This would not constitute a case of so-called 'enhanced co-operation' on the EU model. The proposals envisage the development of co-operative agreements beyond the countries that presently comprise the Union or are in course of joining it. In some cases they exhibit a desire for public adoption of a common set of values and even offer texts to which countries may subscribe.

It is not claimed that the items selected in this compilation exhaust the possibilities for the countries of Europe. The manifesto of the Czech ODS mentions both the European Free Trade Area (EFTA) and the European Economic Area (EEA) as possibilities that are worth further examination. The manifesto also refers to the North American Free Trade Agreement (NAFTA), about whose potential there is a growing literature in Britain, but that is beyond our present scope.

The final alternative differs from the others in that instead of proposing to restructure the EU or to develop a different arrangement it sets out ways in which the Council of Europe in Strasbourg set up earlier by the Treaty of London, and still functioning, could be used more extensively.

The originators of these proposals stand united in a belief that we shall do better to grasp the hands of our neighbours in friendship than in handcuffs.

1

Europe of Many Circles: Constructing a Wider Europe

Richard Body

The EC suffers from three handicaps in seeking to end European divisions. As a supranational authority it can function only by taking away a great deal of power from member states; as a customs union it has become inward-looking; its membership is exclusive. While there is much the peoples of Europe should do together only seldom will it be desirable for them for them to act as one. There are circles of interest that include some nations and exclude others; these circles overlap and some means is needed to co-ordinate them. Convergence of interests is the only basis for international co-operation and all the interests of any one country are not shared with the same countries. The circles of interest of Britain and France, for example, include countries outside Europe but they are not the same countries.

The EC works on the assumption that there is only one circle of interest for all its members. There were many common interests among its six founding members but with its growth the likelihood of divergence has increased faster. It is time to assess whether supranationality has been effective and particularly to note the tactics employed by those who are working to bring about a federal United States of Europe. They understand that the great majority of the people of Western Europe are averse to this goal and have to be brought to agree to each successive step towards it for some plausible and pragmatic reason. But there is no going back on each step.

There are only two roads for nation-states to go when they want to work together, the supranational and the international. In Europe the first will lead either to a megastate or a federal structure; the second to co-ordination in overlapping circles of interest. The supranational road has produced a 'democratic deficit' whereby legislation - which cannot be amended in national Parliaments - is prepared behind closed doors. This will be intolerable but it would be impossible for the European Parliament to represent and be properly accountable to the electorate.

Europe; twelve or many more?

Europe is not now, any more than she has ever been, an homogeneous entity. She is so diverse and contains so many countries that it is difficult to say with any certainty how many there are. There are two ways to position all the different circles of interest that these countries share, either concentric or overlapping. The first is the way envisaged by those seeking to build a deeper Europe, with a core consisting of the twelve members of the EC, EFTA members a little further out and all the other countries at the outer circle. The core is where the decisions are made and power is concentrated. In the alternative pattern circles represent interests which are capable of being treated co-operatively by countries for their common benefit, trade and defence being among the most frequent historically. This pattern is not as rigid as the other and permits self-determination, each country deciding for itself whether to co-operate with others in any specific area of interest.

The weakness of the concentric approach is that all countries are obliged to support any single policy adopted within the circle to which they belong even when they have no interest, for example pollution of the Rhine or Danube, which is of no interest to distant countries. To secure agreement to any policy in the Council of Ministers requires a great deal of horse-trading in which those countries without a direct interest are drawn in by the promise of benefit elsewhere. The result is a sludgy amalgam.

Only two roads to go

There is a common belief that nation-states cause wars, but there is nothing inherent in them that inclines them to invade a neighbour, though there is a danger when big states are alongside smaller ones. There is also a belief that the nation-state is an obsolete relic but this is to ignore the examples of successful modern states that have no intention of giving up their status. The nation-state is no more than a unit of self-government, which can group together with others for common objectives either internationally or supranationally and in no other way.

This is because the characteristics of the nation-state are the powers to make its own laws, to interpret them, to set taxes, to declare war and to make treaties with others, all of which are coercive powers over individuals and together constitute sovereignty. States may either retain these powers, using them in different ways, in which case their co-operation is international, or they can transfer them to another body which will exercise coercion in just one way within all states, i.e. supranationally. Before the Treaty of Accession to the Treaty of Rome treaties were made internationally and did not put a curb on the exercise of the five constitutional powers; since then we and our institutions in Britain have become subordinate in some degree in respect of four of them, retaining the power to declare war. There is no third way in which these powers can be exercised.

Unity and freedom; order and diversity

There is a balance to be struck between man's freedom and his need for social order. How can it be found in a megastate of more than three hundred millon individuals? The idea that man must live in ever enlarging social orders to fulfil his expanding needs is falsified by the experience of numerous small states with high levels of individual prosperity and quality of life, states that show not the slightest inclination to amalgamate. The balance between freedom and unity has to be struck, if it is to be generally acceptable, within a reasonably homogeneous community and this balance will be different in different communities. Small ones have the advantage and it is not easy to see how balance might be achieved in a megastate. In a small state the ordinary citizen can be heard more easily, while in a great one the more likely he is to feel impotent. The fewer the inhabitants the fewer the conflicting interests and minorities are more likely to exercise influence. A European megastate will be in danger of putting unity where freedom belongs and freedom where unity should be.

Small is economic, too.
Customs Union or Free Trade Area

So small is democratic but if a huge supranational union leaves most people feeling powerless would a larger economy provide benefits to set against that feeling? The evidence from European countries outside the EC suggests not, for their economies have not evidently been damaged by exclusion despite what the Norwegians, for example, were told when they had a referendum on entry. Large-scale businesses can go wrong in a big way and large protected markets can induce managerial sloth. Freedom of choice for consumers is max-imised in a free trade area as opposed to a customs union, which is by definition protectionist and has to be centrally reg-ulated at the supranational level, the point at which major multinational companies can exert lobbying power. What small companies need is markets of an appropriate size for the scale of their production. Large-scale economies incur costs that simply do not have to be met in small economies and large enterprises suffer from a law of diminishing productivity to offset economies of scale. The same is true for central regula-tion of the market, which becomes less effective the greater the integrated market becomes.

The customs union lay at the heart of the Treaty of Rome but the international negotiating power it provides is of benefit to member states only as far as their trading interests converge. When it deprives a country's consumers of products that they would prefer to have, such as New Zealand dairy products in the case of Britain, it does that country a disservice. The rea-son for the European customs union was that it was an essen-tial stepping stone to the eventual federal union.

The centrepiece of the customs union is the Common Agricultural Policy, which sets out to change the venue of food production from where it is economically the most efficient to where it is less so. In addition to damaging the interests of con-sumers the policy has been particularly disastrous for Third World farmers by depriving them of export possibilities. On top of this damage, which was always integral to the policy, the encouragement of intensive food production systems has been ecologically damaging in Europe itself.

Some overlapping circles

Environmental policy is today an obvious candidate for co-operation between countries, which it was not when the EC was founded. The Treaties now provide for it but it does not seem that there is sufficient convergence of interest for it to be agreed and - more important - enforced in the member states. Environmental policy actually has to extend wider that the EC yet in the East some of the worst polluters cannot afford to raise their standards.

Among other co-operative areas patents should be remarked. Patent co-operation is very necessary, works very well and does so on an inter-governmental basis extending beyond the EC.

Non-tariff barriers, which are of interest well beyond the EC under the General Agreement on Tariffs and Trade (GATT), continue to be regarded in some countries as deserving of preservation, ie there is insufficient convergence of interest to do away with them entirely. In a partnership of nation-states two or more could be encouraged to reach an agreement by means of benefits specific to themselves, ie to form a common interest. Anti-dumping laws are perfectly capable of being managed by countries for themselves.

Other examples of potential and actual co-operation can be identified such as a single market, Concorde, coal and steel, Western European Union, the Alps, energy conservation, acid rain, the North Sea, food safety and animal welfare.

Circles of conflict

Just as there are areas of common interest that can be handled by means of overlapping circles there are areas in which inter-ests conflict and in which common policy cannot appropriate-ly be developed. One such is agriculture, an area of the EC in which there is a great distinction between North and South. Modern intensive methods are capable of grievous environmental damage in the former but it has not occurred in the latter so that no policy is required there to protect the environment. At the same time the crops grown in the Mediterranean countries are quite different from those in the North so that a common policy is scarcely practical and attempts to devise centrally a list of guaranteed prices would create an obvious conflict of interest.

There is also a conflict of interest between consumers and producers of food in which the existing Common Agricultural Policy favours the latter, effectively denying consumers the opportunity to buy food on the world market. It might be possible in a small country to devise an agricultural policy to satisfy both of them but on the scale of the EC it is neither practicable nor desirable.

There is also a potential circle of conflict over currency. If the currency of one country is allowed to float against the currencies of others it can adjust to reflect and correct differences in their economic structures and performance. If they have one currency their interests conflict and attempts to resolve the situation can result only in more taxation and central direction of resources.

Pragmatic Europe: Economic Commission for Europe

The ECE was set up after the Second World War under the auspices of the United Nations to co-ordinate economic reconstruction. Its members are thirty two European countries. It is little known because it seeks to achieve co-operation between governments and therefore operates where national interests are sufficiently convergent to permit consensus, ie unexcitingly. Unlike the EC it has no need for expenditure on public relations but it exchanges ideas with the Commission of the EC on a regular basis. It is the wishes of the sovereign member governments that determine the activities of the ECE.

Among the areas in which it has been effective are inland transport, covering roads, rail and waterways, the development of trade, particularly the examination of non-tariff barriers and the design of trade data. It has also worked on an Overall Economic Perspective and combined this with environmental considerations, specifically air and water pollution and waste, and with the study of trends in energy use.

Churchill's vision: the Council of Europe

The Council is an organization for co-operation between the nation-states of Europe. It was set up in 1949 at the instigation of Winston Churchill and resolved then that there should be a European Assembly of Parliamentarians and a Court of Human Rights. Membership is open to any country in Europe that recognises the rule of law and guarantees to its people the enjoyment of human rights and fundamental freedoms. Its existence testifies that there are some circles of interest that encompass most of Europe and that governments can achieve results by their co-operation without a merger. The Assembly does not pretend to legislate nor does it tax, both of these activities being reserved to national Parliaments.

The areas in which the Council has been active include human rights, social and economic affairs, and the environment. It operates by means of resolutions setting out the measures each country should take and conventions which bind those members that sign them. Each convention thus identifies a circle of interest within which countries may decide whether or not to take part.

Towards a wider Europe

A wider EC should open its doors to every country considering itself European. Limits on membership would have the disadvantage of excluding countries from playing a part in a circle of interest to which they naturally belong, thereby weakening the power of the other countries in the circle to achieve fully the purpose of their co-operation. While an open Europe would militate against an integrated union of member states, it would strengthen the cohesion of each group of countries. Secondly, a wider Community would recognise that, far from being an homogeneous entity, Europe has such a diverse range of interests that unity would be neither necessary nor feasible. Instead, the different interests that groups of countries have in common need to be identified, and only when it is seen that those interests converge should an attempt be made to agree a common policy or a common programme of action. Thirdly, it is the people themselves, through their elected representatives, that are best qualified to assess the importance of their interests. The fewer the number of people that an elected parliamentarian represents, the less chance there is of a minority interest being overlooked. Bio-regional parliaments [for an area with natural boundaries] may, therefore, be the ideal but in the meanwhile nothing larger than the existing national parliaments should decide whether new laws ought to be passed or new taxes imposed to enable a common policy to be put into effect. Fourthly, as many of Europe's problems have a dimension that stretches beyond the Continent and often around the world, a wider Community should strive to avoid damaging the interests of countries outside. Unfortunately, none of these four principles actuate the EC as it is now.

Europe on a human scale

Europe on a human scale must be something radically different from the dream of the supranationalists. The Community must embrace all of Europe, for environmental and human needs cannot be met on a lesser scale. It must be an open Europe, for a Europe that is commercially isolationist in pursuit of the goal of self-sufficiency is manifestly not fulfilling the human needs that are better satisfied in the markets of the world. And it must be a democratic Europe. Small, or comparatively small, nation-states should decide for themselves what is most appropriate for themselves; and when they decide for themselves that their interests converge with one or more neighbouring states, then a circle of interest can be formed and within that circle they can act together for the common advantage of the people who live in the circle.

Europe has many overlapping circles. That we are failing to employ the means to identify them and the mechanisms to act within them is a sad commentary on how far the idea of European co-operation has moved away from serving the interests of ordinary people.

[Editor's Note: At the time of publication there was a European Community of twelve nations. Subsequent changes have not affected the argument]

2

A Europe Of Nations: Conclusions

The European Research Group

1. Eastward enlargement must be a priority for the EU, with the Visegrad states joining by 1st January 2000 and firm calendars drawn up for other democratic countries wishing to join. This will necessitate profound structural changes to existing EU institutions.

2. Consent and flexibility must underpin European integration, with different groups of states able to co-operate in different areas of policy within the nexus of a free market.

3. All powers should be assumed to rest with national governments unless explicitly stated otherwise in the Treaties. The ambiguous principle of subsidiarity must be replaced by a new formula which explicitly reserves for national governments all areas of policy which cannot be shown directly to affect the internal affairs of other Member States.

4. This principle should further be incorporated, as applicable, in the constitutions of the Member States. Lists should be drawn up to clarify the areas of policy covered, including law, taxation, local government, industrial policy and foreign affairs.

5. The European Commission should be reduced to the role of a civil service carrying out the will of elected ministers. It must lose the right to initiate legislation.

6. The European Parliament must be prevented from competing for power with national parliaments. It should focus simply on scrutinising the work of the Commission.

7. The European Court of Justice must be strictly confined to a specific judicial role interpreting the plain text of the Treaties.

8. The doctrine of the 'occupied field' must be abandoned and the *acquis communautaire* made subject to continuous revision.

9. The Articles which provide for monetary union should be removed from the Treaties. A single currency would come about only through natural evolution with the full consent of all participating nations.

10. Measures must be taken to reduce the EU budget and by stages to return responsibility for agricultural policy to the Member States.

11. The WEU should be decoupled from the institutions of the European Union and remain purely under the control of its member governments.

[Editor's Note: the ERG comprises parliamentarians of twenty-eight Centre-Right parties in twenty countries. Its Conclusions, of which an original summary appears above, were accompanied by detailed proposals for amending the European Union Treaties]

3

The Breakdown of Europe

Richard Body

The ultimate danger now facing the European Union is that of disintegration. It is a process that for decades has been producing more and more states in the world because ordinary people wish to govern themselves and it would be surprising if it did not spread to Europe. Ordinary Europeans have never shared the enthusiasm of their leaders for political union.

At the same time as globalisation is tending to homogenize the world there is at work a counter-tendency for cultural diversity to find political expression in devolution. We have seen how centralisation can give rise to centrifugal forces and these are sometimes very violent. They, rather than nation-states, have accounted for most of the wars since 1945.

Markets on the global scale have disbenefits as well as benefits but it is not the case that only large political units are capable of dealing with them. This is a view from the past, when states protected their own economies by tariffs and other barriers, but nowadays political borders are economically less important. It is generally recognised that governmental interference in trade beyond a very modest level is likely to do more harm than good. When it comes to dealing with powerful transnational corporations a multiplicity of small countries can do better in defending their interests than one super-state that needs to be lobbied in only one place.

The larger the state the more do minorities become impotent and mass majorities are swayed by emotion. Government becomes remote and individuals alienated as decisions are made to forward the interests of an undifferentiated mass. When countries are not allowed to be diverse their peoples will lose their sense of participation in their self-government.

Europe out of control

The love of power has frequently been the motive for bringing Europe under a single rule. The reason there is a democratic deficit in Europe is that the powers of countries have been taken from them to the European Union whose centralised authorities are not subject to democratic control. Governments sit together in secret to produce legislation in ever-widening areas and making more use of the European Parliament will do nothing to improve accountability and reduce the deficit. An MEP cannot be sensitive to the needs of 500,000 constituents and any one of them will have little say in electing him. In earlier days there was at least a common patriotic concern for the good of the country but such feelings are today downplayed by federalists. The result is that they are replaced by a narrow, selfish interest, but in the end this will not satisfy people and their emotional longings could break Europe apart.

There is already great popular hostility at the sheer inefficiency of EU policies, for example in agriculture and fisheries. The direct cost of large-scale bureaucracy, which grows exponentially as the state grows and thus takes a growing proportion of resources to sustain it, must become a source of conflict. At the same time disparities between and within countries that are all part of a single unit can lead to feelings of envy and even hate. If this is a problem now it will be much worse with enlargement. There are already signs of strain within the larger member states of the EU with regional self-assertion. European Union attempts to take advantage of this by a regional policy that will diminish nation states for the benefit of the Union and regions simply will not meet people's needs unless the Union's own authority is dramatically limited. Most people do not show any enthusiasm for the 'European ideal' despite the fortune that has been spent on propaganda. They were originally led to believe that they would become richer without giving up political independence; it was a false prospectus and if we find ourselves in economic decline, as we might well do, there will be powerful demands for autonomy.

Another Europe for the electronic age

Because of the telecommunications revolution the European super-state is obsolete before its structure has been completed. Individuals can spread their views to vast audiences and form alliances with others who have the same interest. Networks will entwine and overlap and encourage migration so that people can live alongside others who share their outlook and interests. People will be able to choose in which country to live and will make their choice on the basis of the differences between them.

The diffusion of power brought about by telecommunications will give minorities political strength, linking up to form coalitions as often as they may wish. Digital technology will make it possible for people to conduct political debates for themselves instead of through representatives. This sort of democracy will be the more effective the smaller and more homogeneous the state concerned.

This state of affairs will be entirely contrary to the ambitions of European federalists; before we go any further down their path we should take a hard look at the sort of world we are really going to be living in a few years from now.

As if people mattered

Structures to settle conflicts of interest between states can be either international or supranational. The former leaves sovereignty with nations who retain the powers of making laws and raising taxes. There are many examples of such international bodies, which depend on the backing of member states which is in turn dependent on their people willing them to succeed.

A supranational structure by contrast takes over law-making, taxation and sovereignty. This is the direction of federal union, the path adopted by the European Union. It is worth looking at the fate of previous federations before we become totally committed. Most, not all, federal unions are doomed, e.g. the Soviet Union, Yugoslavia, the West Indies and Central Africa. Those that work, such as Germany and Australia, do so because they are culturally and linguistically single nations. The United States survives, though its unity was severely tested by a civil war, because the union possesses a carefully balanced constitution which leaves appreciable powers with the states. In Europe there is no limit on the powers that may be transferred to Brussels from the very disparate member countries. An even better exemplar is Switzerland, which has survived for centuries as twenty- two tiny cantons, each of which has more autonomy than an American state and none of which is in a position to dominate the others. If the European Union could be turned into a scaled up version of Switzerland there might be some hope for it.

So far from a single currency being necessary to build prosperity in Europe there is much to be said for multiple currencies. This is just one example of the need for the European Union to change some of its most cherished presumptions. It should recognise that small political units are likely to be more humane and efficient than large ones. They should suffer interference only for some clearly proved benefit, benefit that is for the people and not for politicians, bureaucrats and large corporations. The protection of the environment is one such case because pollution crosses frontiers and it will quickly be seen that the European Union is too small to tackle it. For such purposes enlargement to the East is essential but to try to do it with the present structure would be overwhelmingly difficult. Most of the necessary adjustments would in any case be greatly to our benefit, such as the abandonment of the Common Agricultural Policy and of the constitution of the Union as a customs union rather than a free trade area. In short we ought already to be auditing the Union structures to decide which are beneficial and which are not.

We could do worse than look at the Council of Europe, the Economic Commission for Europe and the Conference on Security and Co-operation in Europe to see how far they could take us. All of them work inter-governmentally. The result is that with them power stays with the peoples of Europe.

If these three are capable of promoting and co-ordinating the cross-frontier co-operation of Europe's peoples why do we need the European Union, limited as it is to only part of Europe? Logic suggests it is unnecessary. If it is to be kept it must be radically reformed, for in its present form it is obsolete. The whole concept belongs to an earlier period in history, before the coming of the global market and the information revolution made political boundaries largely irrelevant to economic activity. In the context of trade the European Union has become not just superfluous but positively harmful, for individual states need to retain some control over the effects of inter-state trade in case parts of their economies need temporary protection, the most effective form of protection being a separate currency.

The present European Union is both too small and too large. It is too small because in the economic sphere it faces worldwide commercial and technological forces that it can never hope to control. It is too large because people are happier, more fulfilled and better governed when the unit of government is scaled down. The marvels of the new age will empower the people. They will break down Europe.

4

Pour les états-généraux de la souveraineté nationale

Alain Bournazel and Etienne Tarride

The France we want

France is a nation and it is also a European nation. This is not simply by virtue of its geography but also because of the major role it has played in the diverse and fruitful history of Western civilisation. National feeling in France has never expressed itself by a withdrawal into isolationism, but at the same time France has consistently fought off every kind of external domination.

In every continent the nation-state model has been adopted and with their growing number, evident in the United Nations, it is the concert of nations that commands the international scene. This does not mean that the idea of nationhood is easy to grasp, for it varies as much as the nations themselves. It is the nation that gives to every people the collective memory that underlies the thread of its history and provides a signpost in its journey of trial and error towards the future.

France is a world power by virtue of its history and its place on the international scene. The traces of its empire, the widespread use of its language, its place on the Security Council and its global economic performance all testify to its standing. What is more, its intellectual and moral influence far surpass its economic and financial potential.

France is a Republic, one of the first. Republicanism involves democratic representation of the people by universal suffrage but, in France at any rate, it cannot be reduced to the mere mechanics of democracy. Above all it involves a value system that shapes the totality of our society and reflects its national identity. These values are based on the supreme place of the political form of power and organisation over all others in a society.

The principles that formerly underpinned the Republic are today faced with a radical challenge, one possessing an air of inevitability before which our leaders can only surrender: this challenge is that of globalisation, which is attacking the framework of nations. The current form of European construction is the agency by which France is being drawn to submit to globalisation, while the euro is the pretext for doing nothing to redress the deflation of the French economy over the last 25 years.

The great problem is that of unemployment, growing steadily despite all the efforts to contain it. It is both an economic catastrophe and an assault on the cohesion of French society, which is becoming divided between two extremes. On the one hand there are front-rank enterprises producing considerable profits, a substantial positive balance of payments and paying good salaries. At the other end of the scale there are run-down estates of poverty and despair, where unemployment is the bleak inheritance that passes down the generations. Everything that has been tried has failed because it seeks to ameliorate the consequences without tackling the root cause. What we need is a different economic policy.

France is constructed around the State but the State has been devalued. Yet only the State can produce the fundamental reforms that will ensure the survival of the nation and it needs itself to be reformed. It should not seek to do everything and has in fact been successfully decentralised in recent years, thus bringing into play great reserves of initiative in the regions. But it should not seek to pass off its own responsibilities to others, especially not to the European Union. It now has to set out a strategy for the future and muster the energies of the nation for major programmes. If it relies on the market to look after the short-term it still has to look after the long-term itself.

National unity must be restored and unemployment brought right down. It must be seen not as inevitable but as an opportunity. The Maastricht criteria call for a policy based on monetary balances, a policy which takes no account of employment, and transferring to the euro will not resolve the problem of unemployment. It is neither a European nor a global problem, even if other countries suffer from it; it has specific characteristics in each country and each must arrive at an employment policy that draws on its own resources.

The challenge of modernity in a dangerous world has to be met by openness to the world. We have to adapt to world changes and economic power is the one means to underpin all we want our country to do. French society needs a collective project to focus its vision of the future. The EU has not the capability to produce it and we should remember that it is those parts of the world that promote new technology that have the lowest rates of unemployment.

To ensure that the economic and social aspects of policy are in balance requires greater popular participation. This calls in turn for a system of education that enables individuals to act as citizens and encourages them to go on learning throughout life.

Modern democracy demands direct discussion between governors and the governed, which means access to major channels of communication. The sensible use of the referendum enables the direction of government policy to be aligned with the popular will and it is a pity there are not more of them. It is for us to devise the structures of participative democracy of the 21st century.

We should not succumb to the illusion that the great changes of recent years mean that there is now no role for a France grown too small to do other than submit to the world market and to the direction of supranational bodies. The world is not about to become pacific and the voice of France will need to be heard in it. We have not lost our capacity for creation and renewal.

The Europe we want
The foundations of a genuine Europe

The right of every nation to exercise its veto on any European measure which seriously damages its vital interests, a right which since the crisis of 1965 has been known as the Luxembourg compromise, remains a compelling principle in the building of Europe. Europe must be built and Europeans must adopt common policies to tackle the major problems that confront them, but no common policy should fail to respect the true interests of each of the nations that make up Europe. This principle marks out a more difficult route than the paths adopted by those who would sacrifice everything to a supranational Europe or those whose nationalism forbids any form of European structure. The idea of a Europe based on permanent negotiation between its nations is in no way constraining; on the contrary it is our belief that it will permit more rapid progress than the current federalist idea.

At present every decision put into the hands of the Community constitutes an ireversible transfer of sovereignty. It is virtually impossible to go back on the decisions of European bodies, which are all too likely to regard themselves as endowed with a general mission that permits them to go beyond what was originally required of them. This rigidity in Europe means that every crisis puts its very existence at risk, thereby forcing the hands of its leaders to do anything to avoid an explosion. This situation is not healthy.

The European debate is not just between the extremes but involves, on both sides, people of good will and good faith who do not have the same idea of Europe nor the same idea of France. Because the world is moving, fortunately, in the direction of larger but peaceful groups the necessary common rules will be accepted much more easily than some believe. At the same time it would be mad to try to create some kind of centralised, domineering super-state precisely when the defects of this sort of organization are recognised and combatted everywhere.

Our opposition to what is mistakenly nowadays called Europe is that Europeans are not putting together a political structure but permitting the installation of a strange machine steered on auto-pilot and one which links itself to yet more machines, of which the most notorious is 'economic globalisation'. We are told that the market is king and that its supremacy is inevitable. But in Europe as elsewhere it must be democracy that prevails over the market, even if the latter is both necessary and beneficial. We have no intention of abandoning government of the people by the people even if that is not in the interest of the global financial market, even if the great European monetary market has made up its mind otherwise. The building of Europe must supplement French democracy, not strengthen the hands of elites or financial powers of whatever origin. It is precisely because we believe that a European organization of a particular form would help to safeguard French democracy that we favour it.

Europe is run by the Commission, a body which is unaccountable in the political sense and whose output shows not the least care for the reality that shapes people's lives or the interests of Europe's peoples. It is governed by the dogma of the market as king against which nothing else counts. Like all totalitarian ideologies it will collapse one day. Better not to allow it to be set up.

The building of Europe should proceed on certain conditions. The first of them is the scrupulous respect of national sovereignty. The sovereign nation is the only structure within which democracy can be exercised. It has long been the case that the verdicts reached by universal suffrage have not been seriously challenged. There is nothing inevitable about this; indeed it is something of a miracle that has been brought about by the will of people to live in common, and it is only that same will which enables some part of them to accept heavy taxation. Then there is willingness to respect judicial decisions and this also is due to their being delivered in the name of the sovereign French people.

The second condition is the right to have decisions taken at the level they should be taken and with due regard for the interests and needs of those who will suffer by or profit from them. Subsidiarity is often proclaimed but rarely put into practice.

The third is that nations retain at least the possibility of confronting events or shocks, whether political, economic or social. Without a principle of reversibility Europe could face disaster; indeed with it progress could actually be improved, for decisions are being held up because nations fear to make them if they cannot later put the machine into reverse. The Europe of the europhiles has no notion of making a trial of anything. Matters would be quite different if nations could, under appropriate conditions, recover some portion of sovereignty. For example, in the Single Market they have not the least power over competition law. A proposal to use public money to support a bank or major concern has to get past a Commissioner in Brussels, who will insist on conditions, even on privatisation. It would be better if the country concerned, following due procedure, could suspend the competition rules. The possibility of restoring a national currency would have made the Maastricht Treaty much more acceptable.

The fourth condition is that under no circumstances should there be any attack on national languages or defence arrangements.

Restructuring the foundations

Given the nature of the European institutions a thorough-going reform of the system is what is required. Its outstanding characteristic is the total unaccountability of all the possessors of real power, the absence of any democratic control. The true power at the heart of Europe should be assigned to the one institution which has some slight democratic credibility, the Council of Ministers. It is the Council that must be charged with initiating enactments. The Commission should become what it always should have been, an administrative organ without any political authority.

The European Parliament should be the seat for great debates on general policy, particularly foreign policy. These should be widely disseminated in the media and Parliamentary controversies should have the fullest public airing.

National Parliaments on the other hand should be responsible for the amendment and adoption of official documents emanating from Europe. The clandestine manner in which Europe is being built at present must be done away with. Every document of importance must be the subject of public debate. This reform would settle the irritating question of unanimous or majority voting; the necessity of ratification in national Parliaments will make it possible to proceed by simple majority without risk. We are not fond of unanimity because it opens the door to bargaining, blackmail and secrecy. It helps to make it impossible to overturn harmful European arrangements if only one of our partners benefits from them. Our proposal to empower national Parliaments to adopt enactments put forward at the European level will require amendment of the French Constitution. We suggest that this constitutional reform should be made the subject of a referendum for we have nothing to fear from an opposition which will certainly be furious but will openly show itself to be reactionary.

The excessive integration promoted by the European institutions is accompanied by an excess of caution in some respects. European organized crime has existed for a long time, whereas a European police system still falters. Europol should be strengthened and become a genuine European body for common action, able to work freely in every country.

Similarly with protecting the environment. Catastrophes and pollution do not respect frontiers; why should the bodies charged with preventing them or tackling their consequences respect them?

Health is another area which calls for much stronger co-operation. It is absurd that across Europe there should be separate medical research budgets and unharmonized hospital systems.

It is essential that the EU develop a common immigration

policy. We already have freedom of movement, which will be extended with the accession of applicant countries. The procedures governing visits and settlement in any EU nation must be completely harmonized, otherwise the most liberal countries run the risk of being swamped while the most restrictive will find themselves powerless and their ostensible legal position bypassed.

Firmly against the euro

The arguments in this debate have been well rehearsed. It is a gamble. Not a week goes by without our being told by the europhiles that the euro will be a world currency to rival the dollar and will afford Europe a control of monetary policy that she does not now possess. In a regime of floating currencies - and nobody is suggesting a return to fixed rates - the euro will certainly suffer volatility to an extent of which we have little experience in Europe. Its objective, established by the financial powers and their political allies, is to enfeeble completely the people's representatives for the profit of economic interests. The benefits asserted for the euro are just gambles and even if they succeed will not bring much satisfaction to most Europeans. If in the end they fail the results will be terrifying.

Maastricht has produced a system in which the participating nations are depriving themselves of a very powerful instrument, the moderate injection of liquidity into the economy or a reasonable increase of public debt. This is an archaic recipe which leaves wages and salaries the only major means of adjustment of the economic situation.

It need not have been like this. The European Monetary System was not essentially unsound but it was unambitious. We are sure our leaders did not seek to improve it precisely because it did not set national sovereignty aside, although it limited it. Properly managed it could have been strengthened to enable us to meet the grave danger arising from unlimited floating of major currencies against each other. In these circumstances the retention and development of a common currency could well be envisaged, a currency which could readily have replaced national currencies for transactions within the Community. This would have offered the same benefits as the single currency without abolishing the room for manoeuvre required by national authorities, without turning asymmetric shocks into catastrophes and, above all, without depriving citizens of broad ranges of political choice henceforth reserved to central bankers.

What is to be done? What is to be avoided?

There are two reasons why the europhiles began their assault on the powers of states with money; their own training and their privileged allies. The nature of the latter is well understood but the essential motivation has been the training received by almost all eurocrats. Because of it they are convinced that today the overriding power is financial power. This does not mean that they began by making a study of money. What really inspires the eurocrat is power itself.

Even if monetary unification has transferred substantial power the irreversible Europeanisation of our countries remains to be completed, for example in foreign policy and defence. They will use the same tactics.

For a eurocrat the first protective requirement is to obfuscate. All the preliminaries to Maastricht remained completely unknown to the bulk of the population and it will be the same thing with foreign policy and defence. The second need is disguise. The object is to have people believe that what is is not, as when Jacques Chirac described Maastricht as a very small step in the right direction when he could not have supposed for a moment that this was truly the case. Remember how we were told that just the period from Maastricht to the coming into force of the euro would create millions upon millions of jobs, especially in France. The third device on which they must rely, and one which we hear today, is that it is all too late. Just at the point when the eurocrats deign to reveal that the euro is not a minor technical measure or an immediate guarantee of paradise, when the problems become apparent, it is well understood that everything is committed and there is no going back.

Towards no defence

Clearly a decisive battle will take place over defence policy. The eurocrats will inevitably seek to apply the finishing touches by creating an integrated European defence. We cannot accept this for defence is national or it is nothing. All discussion in any European body must therefore be completely open. It would be completely irresponsible for a treaty to be prepared on the sly either to denuclearise France in order to create an integrated conventional European army or to place the French nuclear deterrent under a command which is not exclusively French or to leave France with only its nuclear force.

The other tactic will also be put to work. Right to the last minute there will be a pretence that the agreements coming out of secret discussions in no way mean what the anti-Europeans want them to mean. We should remember that secret preliminary talks are a proof of organized deceit. Defence is a clear example but our reasoning applies to other subjects, particularly foreign policy.

However, foreign policy is nevertheless an area in which a real political Europe could and should come into being. This is demonstrated by the complete inability of European governments to work out a desirable future for Bosnia and the means of its implementation. Europe needs to debate the great problems of the world, to define its own interest and its goals and the means it intends to deploy to promote them. If that turns out to be impossible, if in the face of reality Europe cannot arrive at an agreement which goes beyond a simple statement of principles or pious wishes the situation would be very serious.

Europe needs to be independent of the United States. A subordinate policy will give us nothing. A policy run by a rootless cabal will never be able to take the necessary initiatives and will never be able to break away from the position of second fiddle to America. It is precisely because we believe that the interests and the desires of the peoples of Europe are the same or consonant and that elected governments are the best interpreters of these interests and desires that we judge the procedure of dialogue and permanent negotiation to be the one which will bear witness to the reality of Europe.

Why Europe?

The construction of Europe is vital for the survival of our countries in the 21st century. It is probably the only way to offer the French, particularly French youth, a genuine political programme, a collective enthusiasm to stand against the sullen cynicism that we perceive today. The Europe of Maastricht and Amsterdam cannot do this. It is nothing but a powerful device for creating a world ruled solely by markets. Our nations are by no means powerless alone but are more powerful together. We want a united Europe which gives the market its due place but no more.

5

Europe - Démocracie ou Super-Etat

Georges Berthu

Democracy in danger

Democracy is in danger because it is being taken away from nations by the European Union but cannot be replaced at the European level. This is the fundamental reason why the Union finds itself today in a blind alley. The solution is to abandon its monolithic ambitions and to reshape European co-operation as a network.

The paradox of the super-state

The European institutions are moving ever further from national control but their growing power, far from reinforcing the whole, results only in weakness. This is the paradox. At the same time the conditions necessary for the operation of democracy cannot be put in place at the European level, so that the attempt to legitimise Brussels with a democratic add-on is bound to fail. 'European democracy' is just a fiction, no more than an empty shell. The badly conducted super-state is being distanced from people's expectations and has become the plaything of pressure groups and bureaucrats. Instead of strengthening Europe it weakens it as can be seen in the case of the common commercial policy for goods. International trade negotiations conducted by the European Commission and divorced from national control have proved disastrous for Europe. The anti-democratic system that we have has so many levers in its hands that it is fairly secure despite lacking any popular base. Powerful economic forces sustain the supranational direction of the construction of Europe by favouring the unified commercial legislation that suits their purposes in spite of the fact that national interests differ. At the same time national governments quietly enjoy their ability to conduct their business without being exposed to scrutiny.

A short history of decline

The history of Europe since the Treaty of Rome, contrary to what one might believe, has not proceeded in a linear fashion. In the first stage the supranational conception of the Community was a response to the apparent need for Western Europe to come together in the face of pressure from the Eastern bloc and it was this that permitted the development of the anti-democratic 'Monnet method' in the Coal and Steel Community. It was put forward as a first step towards European federation and was placed in the hands of an explicitly supranational High Authority. There was no democratic mandate and the intention was for supranationality to grow naturally from the fact of association. The 'Monnet method' was repeated with the creation of the European Economic Community but thereafter the attitude of General de Gaulle tilted the institutional balance towards a Europe of Nations. Effectively the 'Monnet method' was held at bay until the Single Act of 1987, which in the interest of creating a single market greatly extended qualified majority voting in the economic field. It was a tragic mistake to extend the Community's competences in this way without strengthening democratic controls. It is from that time that the process of 'meshing together' has accelerated, with the progressive dispossession of national democracies. This trend was reinforced by Maastricht which, when it made provision for a single currency beyond the control of national democracies, showed once more that it was impossible to endow the European institutions with any real democratic legitimacy. The European Central Bank, on the other hand, acquired real monetary sovereignty without any accountability. Amsterdam did nothing to close the gap when it extended the competences of Brussels, opened up the possibility of depriving a member state of its rights - but not its obligations - and affirmed the superiority of the European Court of Justice over all national courts.

In the 'Monnet method' nobody starts with the fundamental question 'What sort of European co-operation do the peoples want?'

The institutional bias

From the beginning the draftsmen of the Treaties introduced an institutional bias that angled decisions in a supranational direction and away from reluctant national democracies. Within this primary bias lay another, the tendency for the construction of the super-state to go in a monolithic rather than a federal direction. This is what brought about, under the pretext of common European interest, the conferment of extraordinary powers on the institutions most remote from national democracies - the Commission and the Court of Justice. The power of the European Parliament to censure the Commission does nothing to reinforce the rights of nations because the two of them have a common interest, while the power of the Commission as against the European Council is reinforced by its monopoly of the initiation of legislation and its veto over amendment. In the absence of a single European people the Parliament instead of reinforcing the general level of democracy weakens it by introducing confusion and undermining well-rooted national democracies. In 1992 the co-decision power granted to the European Parliament rather than reducing the democratic deficit enabled it to give further support to the federalist ambitions of the Commission and divorced Europe still more from its peoples.

This bias, which national governments sitting in the European Council and national Parliaments could have done more to resist, leads systematically to European decisions that are out of line with the common preferences of the member states. This gives an inbuilt pressure towards the creation of a super-state, despite all the ill-founded denials of the federalists, and one which is more and more a unitary monolith rather than a genuine federation.

Supranational plans

Faced by the challenges of enlargement Brussels has taken preemptive flight. The usual demand for more supranational power to counterbalance increased diversity has been deployed, with proposals for adjusting the number of Commissioners, reweighting the votes of member states and extending qualified majority voting. Grandiloquent proposals have been submitted to the Inter-Governmental Conference on matters such as a European Constitution and a Charter of Fundamental Rights, which is to form the first part of it. Community funds are to be used to promote the development of political parties on a European scale. All this is intended to push national democracies a little further aside and prevent each people from making independently the major decisions that will govern its future. A second chamber of the European Parliament could even bring about the end of the present representation of national governments in the European Council.

The proposal for an 'advance guard' is out of line with the federalist dogma that has pertained hitherto, which insisted that all member states were fully and equally involved in the Union. It is full of danger for France. The operation of qualified majority voting within the 'advance guard' would accelerate supranationality and complete the destruction of member states' sovereignties. It would also set in concrete a Franco-German entente that is in no-one's interest and put it largely in German hands by virtue of the size of its population.

A changing world

The European super-state finds itself ill-suited to deal with the pressures of the modern global economy, a point which nullifies the argument that it alone can supply the weight needed to stand up to them. Cut off from national roots the super-state can easily be seized by pressure groups. Globalisation calls for competitiveness whereas artificial structures lose contact with people and popularly shared values so that they become rule-bound and subject to additional costs; unable for example to correct unwanted side-effects of international trade; the wide distribution of information nullifies authoritarian decisions that are out of touch with the real world - such as the single currency, which is subject not only to the judgements of governments but to those of a large number of actors around the world; the theory of optimal single currency zones is a good example of the need to balance potential benefits of any unification against the likely costs; which all too often are not quantifiable, such as the loss of democracy and beneficial emulation between centres of power.

The existence of shared values, which lessen uncertainty about behaviour, is essential for the proper exercise of democracy: a political community must locate the focus of its political energy at the level at which such values are most closely clustered, that is the nation.

Enlargement to the East reveals at one stroke the contradictions between the rigidity of the super-state and the new world. A system operated on the basis of majorities is unacceptable unless those who participate in it have sufficiently close interests. This leads to the principle that those admitted to the Union have to do so wholly, with all the rights and duties of the others, but it is simply not credible in respect of the current set of applicants. The keyword for resolving the dilemma of enlargement is no longer centralisation but network.

The principles of networks

A bogus alternative is posed by those who say there will be 'a Super-State or nothing'. If the peoples of Europe recover their freedom of decision they will quite naturally take the path of new forms of co-operation based on their values and common interests. There will not be a political void in the face of the market but a search for a new equilibrium between the market and democratic decision-making, so that policy can take into account unquantified social costs. What networks do is to create horizontal links between autonomous power centres, in this case nations. The answer to the question 'Who then takes the common decisions?' is 'the network'. This is not a simple idea for those brought up with the notion of nation-states to grasp. Such states are not themselves networks. The super-state modelled on the nation-state fits people's received ideas and is therefore more visible even to those who do not support it. The network thus needs additional explanation.

The first step will be for nations to determine their own stance by democratic procedures and then to set up links to advance their objectives by allying themselves with partners that have similar needs. The Union would just be one co-ordinating centre among others, having no overriding legitimacy. It will act as a service provider to nations.

By comparison with a super-state a network offers a number of advantages: it avoids any separation from the needs of peoples because it puts democratic majority government at its most effective level; it makes for a better distribution of responsibilities in the same way that private property rights are better than Soviet collectivism; it engages the energies of all more fully because it is not bound to the lowest common denominator of fifteen members; it draws in information more widely; it adapts more flexibly, which is the appropriate response to globalisation; it is not blocked by the need to secure the agreement of fifteen states for treaty changes; it is the key to the dilemma of enlargement, which exists only because of federalism. Finally, network Europe will not be open to the seizure of control by those who are able to put together a blocking minority to direct the centralised institutions, especially by first taking control of the 'advance guard'.

It will be desirable to have some general structure to promote linkages whose remit could go beyond the existing frontiers, thus doing away with the problem of where to fix the frontiers of Europe.

Sovereign partners

Among the cloudy and grandiloquent expressions deployed by federalists we find 'pooled sovereignty'. Put into effect it would be the death knell of national sovereignties, whereas network Europe would constitute a system of sovereignties in partnership. Majority voting, promoted by the Commission to cope with the increasingly divergent interests of more members, becomes less and less satisfactory. For countries and people to live together they have all to accept the common rules; in an open world it is more and more difficult to secure respect for rules not based on free consent. The presumption of majority voting is that debate is brought to an end because all are not in agreement and the minority must be forced to yield, to say goodbye to the wishes of their peoples.

By contrast what we want is a Europe whose peoples display mutual respect and none is obliged to do what it does not want, i.e. a system of unanimity. The European Union should entrench once and for all the Luxembourg Compromise. This would encourage negotiation and compromise, while reducing the power of the Commission. It can be made more flexible by differentiated co-operation, which can take place in a smaller area than that of the whole Union or in a larger one, bringing in third parties. Common foreign and security policy, justice and even the Single Market could be dealt with in this way.

What we need is a new working method, 'open co-ordination' rather than the 'reinforced co-operation' which is the device for the 'advance guard'. The three elements of the former would be partnership, in which the different national democracies make their choices freely, the avoidance of all binding measures of an irreversible character, and freedom in co-operation without submission to a predetermined hierarchical structure.

The institutions of a free Europe

Brussels wants to squeeze all the countries of the continent into its institutions but enlargement puts into question its fundamental objective of a unitary European state. This impasse blocks everything. In fact what is needed is to use some imagination to reshape the EU institutions and to create those of a Greater Europe with the help of just one principle, the lawful primacy of national democracies.

The pattern of freedom for Greater Europe will contain three levels: the Charter of Nations to define the common values of peoples, including respect for their identity and sovereignty and the basics of the network; the Standing Conference of heads of state and governments working by unanimity; and the right of members to engage in variable co-operation.

In the Union the Council of Ministers must recover its leading role, with the Commission as a co-ordinating secretariat which can also be deployed in the service of variable co-operation. The Union must be in practice what it already is in theory an association of nations that respects its members' identities, based on the principles of liberty, democracy and the rule of law. The Council must be at the heart of it, promoting variable co-operation where there is not unanimity, exercising control of the Commission.

Inter-governmental procedure must be improved; national Parliaments must have the right to scrutinise European matters directly; an 'inter-parliamentary democracy' must be put in place, of which a network of national Parliaments will be the best illustration.

Finally, it is essential to revise our own Constitution so as to strengthen our national control over European questions with more extensive resort to referendums.

Europe - Démocracie ou Super-Etat *by Georges Berthu*
F.-X. de Guibert, ISBN 2 86839 711 5

6

Associated, Not Absorbed. The Associated European Area: a constructive alternative to a single European state

Bill Cash MP

Euro-realists have often been accused of offering no constructive alternative to a single European state. This pamphlet answers this charge.

The French and German governments, among others, are seeking changes to the Treaty on European Union to create an 'inner core' of states on a 'fast track' to integration, i.e. European government. This they call 'flexibility' and it is intended to provide two paths to the goal, one fast and one slow. These changes require agreement and thus provide the opportunity for other countries to demand treaty changes allowing for the creation of an alternate grouping: the Associated European Area. The Association would challenge the European Union to become flexible enough to accommodate not merely two tracks, but two different spheres. The countries of Europe would then have a clear choice between these spheres: European government, *via* the inner core, or

European trade and association, *via* the Associated European Area.

The name 'Associated European Area' reflects the inter-governmental nature of the group. Rather than a concentric arrangement, such as is suggested by the 'flexibility' doctrine of an inner core and outer circle, the Association would be non-centric in structure, based upon a narrow set of rules on trade and environmental policy. These would be created and applied through strictly inter-governmental channels. Members would not be party to any of the governmental aspects of the European Union and would avoid the alternative fate of constituting merely the leftovers from the creation of a Franco-German inner core. The Association would thus falsify the view of countries outside the core as laggards and would give them a distinct status and direction of their own.

Treaty changes

Both the Associated European Area and the inner core proposal require treaty changes, which must be unanimous. France and Germany propose that the 'inner core' be subject to qualified majority voting, a change that calls for unanimity in the first place. The treaty amendments to accommodate the Association include the first two below as a minimum, while the third is desirable.

1. An amendment, retrospective in force, allowing the states of the Associated European Area to be subject only to those elements of the *acquis communautaire* (the accumulated body of law governing the European Union) compatible with the Association's ambit of trade and environmental policy.

Obtaining consensus among member states for this amendment would be eased by the fact that France and Germany require an amendment to establish the inner core. To embark regularly on EU projects without including all members they would have to scrap the requirement that every member must accept the *acquis* in full. There is a difference in that the inner core amendment need not apply retrospectively, whereas the Association amendment would have to do so. But treaty changes allowing inner core countries to proceed in their preferred direction are no more legitimate than those to allow Association countries to proceed in theirs.

Current exemptions from sections of the *acquis* take the form of opt-outs. This mechanism is consonant with the 'single sphere' view of the EU. It enables states at best to qualify rather than challenge that single sphere, and the history of opt-outs is that they are soon relinquished. Opt-outs do not extend to applicant states who must, as a condition of accession, accept the *acquis* in full.

The proposed amendment would remove the United Kingdom from all areas of qualified majority voting and responsibilities including aid, agriculture and fisheries would be repatriated.

2. An amendment providing for the right of the Associated European Area freely to conclude trade agreements in the absence of action by the European Union as a whole.

The repeated attempts of the European Commission to secure a free-trade agreement with the NAFTA group were blocked by a single member state: France. This amendment would allow the Association, whilst remaining within the Single Market, to secure its own free-trade agreements in the absence of action by the EU as a whole.

This would require renegotiation of the customs union element of the EU. If the Association abolished trade restrictions with NAFTA the free circulation of goods and services within

EU borders, which is a core element, would be compromised. It would not, however, require the scrapping of the customs union to accommodate this situation, for the union could be qualified in much the same way as the United Kingdom qualifies the free movement of people by retaining independent border controls.

3. An amendment stating that nothing in the *acquis* shall be interpreted as challenging the right of Member states, under their own authority, to withdraw from the European Union. The Treaty of Rome contains no right of exit but if member states are still sovereign it follows that the right of secession must still lie with them. This amendment would make the right of secession explicit for those states that wish to preserve it, whilst allowing those that wish to relinquish the right to do so explicitly rather than, as at present, by legal attrition. Doubtless the issue of secession will one day require clarification and it is wise to provide it now rather than wait for it to become urgent.

Negotiations

Invitations to join the Association would be sent to a number of present members of the EU, to the applicant states and to some European countries that have refused membership. Some present members object to concentric flexibility because they do not welcome the destination to which both the fast and slow lanes are intended to lead. Many of the applicants have already expressed discontent at the current direction of the EU and the Association would relieve them of the burden of the *acquis*.

The Associated European Area will be alleged to amount to withdrawal from the EU. In fact it would allow the issue of Europe to transcend the binary in/out question and shift the debate to the question of where membership can be permitted to take us. Renegotiation is not new in EU history but has gone on regularly. It is just that it has always gone in the direction of further integration, as it is doing now. Because of the trade benefits to other members it is not in their interest to use the Association proposal as an excuse for ejecting the United Kingdom.

Ratification

The treaty to establish the Associated European Area would be the subject of referendums in all signatory countries. It would not be able to evolve beyond the mandate thus given because its ambit would be narrow and for the most part static. Furthermore its treaty should contain a clause requiring any amendments to be passed unanimously at summits held at fixed intervals, so that they could not be manoeuvred to coincide with fluctuations in public opinion. All amendments would be subject to referendums.

European Union institutions

The states of the Associated European Area would withdraw from the supranational institutions of the EU and acquire observer status on them and in the inter-governmental Council of Ministers. They would retain voting rights on the core sections of the *acquis* to which they still subscribed.

The proposed arrangement is no more unwieldy than having an inner core and an outer circle with different versions of the *acquis*.

[Editor's Note: If the Nice Treaty is ratified some of the tactical points made here will be overtaken]

7

Separate Ways

Peter Shore

Alternative futures

There is no inevitability about British membership of the euro and ever-closer union though it is certainly an effective argument put about by Europhiles. Polls show that nevertheless a growing majority of the British people is hostile to abandoning the pound sterling, even though at the same time it believes that we are *bound* to join.

This defeatism needs to be challenged by beginning with the assumptions that underlie the reasons advanced for European Union. The most important of these is the prevention of the wars that ravaged the Continent in the first half of the twentieth century. But German military power, together with that of most European states, has been absorbed in the American-led NATO alliance, which is what has really ensured the peace. It is alliances put together in this way that have traditionally been the means of co-operation between states, not supranational commitments of the kind involved in European Union. These have not even delivered since 1973 the economic growth which formed the argument for membership at that time. The abusive assertions of isolationism and xenophobia that have since appeared just cannot be taken seriously.

There is also the deeper issue of globalisation that is now advanced as the case for integration. World trade has increased immensely, capital is free to move all over the globe in the service of giant, multinational corporations, while the internet is a free zone for the exchange of information. It is said that in the face of this assault on everything traditional about national government there is simply no point in trying to retain a national economic policy. Of course things have changed enormously, including the power of governments to control exchange rates but the argument is much overstated. The basic need in this field is to have floating rates and these are open to the influence of nation-state governments, which can continue to navigate their own macro-economic policies.

In some quarters there has also been a deep emotional hostility to the very idea of the nation-state, buttressed in the past by the attraction of Marxist doctrines that advocate the repudiation of capitalism. Within the present British government the hostility has survived the complete abandonment of the doctrines. It is paradoxical for this to have occurred at a time when the creation of nation-states is a striking and welcome development, one for which there is evidently an imperative demand.

Empires have gone and most people in the world now live in nation-states and show no inclination, outside Western Europe, to give them up. Self-government has an unequalled legitimacy and it is helping to bring about the growth of democracy within states, which in turn is helping to reduce the risk of war. At the same time agreements and treaties between states are endlessly negotiated, the great majority of them concerned with forging trade links, certainly not with building embryo states. It is necessary only to look at North America, Latin America, Asia or Africa to see this.

The continuing impetus to ram together the separate nations and states of Europe springs from the long struggle between France and Germany and the memory of their wars. It does not have the same force for other countries and the Europhile argument that the United Kingdom is a weak and exhausted nation that has no choice but to associate itself with this movement is patently false and absurd.

Inside the European Union - New options

The process of integration is far from coming to an end. It has spread ever more widely and gone ever more deeply and the lines of further advance are clearly marked. Tax harmonization and the development of a Common Foreign Policy, backed up by a European Defence capability are plain to see. At the same time the supranational institutions are to be strengthened and the European Union itself, as distinct from the European Community, is on course to be given a legal personality as an internationally recognised entity. This would enable the EU to take a seat on the UN Security Council, quite possibly in place of the UK and France, and to have a single Diplomatic Service.

This, surely, is what is involved in 'being at the heart of Europe' and yet is completely contrary to the pledges of the British government, for example, on retaining the veto on tax matters and rejecting federation. Where is the escape from this nightmare that is not to amount to yet another and final surrender?

The conventional wisdom is that it is not possible to say 'Yes' to what suits us and 'No' to what doesn't, to 'pick and choose'. But in many ways we have done little else but exercise opt-outs. The British electoral system based on the single constituency was retained for twenty years for elections to the European Parliament. The UK stayed out of the Exchange Rate

Mechanism from 1979 to 1990 and had to be peremptorily withdrawn two years later. It is a practice that resembles the behaviour of France in relation to NATO, when from 1958 it withdrew all its forces from unified commands, expelled NATO HQ from its territory but retained its seat and voice in the NATO Council Chamber.

The development which gives the greatest credence to multi-tier working is the project of enlargement to the East. Twelve states have now applied for membership, all of whom are in principle entitled to it. Great obstacles have to be overcome. Thanks to their history the Eastern economies are unlikely to withstand unrestrained competition, the power of the European Commission to veto state aids, the cost of compliance with the massive quantity of regulation in all fields that constitutes the *acquis communautaire*, all at the same time as adopting the single currency and an open-ended commitment to Political Union.

The burden for the existing member states may seem even heavier. The Common Agricultural Policy, which has bestowed great prosperity on the farmers of France, Germany, Holland and Denmark, remains substantially intact but cannot be extended to the applicant countries without either massive change or a huge increase in costs. The Commission's Agenda 2000 proposals for dealing with the problem, however limited, were simply torn up in favour of French farmers and the status quo. A similar difficulty is evident in the claims that might be made by the applicant countries for regional assistance at the expense of its present recipients. The figures do not add up but there has been no recognition of this within the EU. Any proposal to increase the 'own resources' of the EU to the level required, that is substantially, would be a subject of explosive sensitivity for the member states that would have to provide them. If that were not enough there is the enormously challenging problem of the free movement of labour, which is a basic principle of the EU. The pressure for immigration from the impoverished East cannot be resisted within the terms of the treaties that are the law of the EU.

The negotiation of transitional periods has been the traditional device for tackling accession problems and in this case some of them would have to be very long indeed. Despite denials this would amount to creating a two-tier Europe.

At the same time it has been recognised that the institutional arrangements for managing an EU of fifteen member states and giving each of them appropriate representation cannot be continued with extensive enlargement, which may well not stop at twenty seven. Where does Europe end?

This brings us back to the whole question of a two-tier or a multi-tier Europe. It might be fudged for several years by the device of a prolonged transition period but that cannot last. Enlargement spells the end of the strategic aim of 'ever closer union' and requires a much looser association. The United Kingdom would not be alone in pressing for a long-term, probably permanent, two-tier or multi-tier Europe, rather than a temporary one. Many member states are already half-convinced that this is now the most satisfactory option - indeed the only realistic option available.

The Treaty of Amsterdam introduced the concept of 'closer co-operation' to enable some member states to pursue new integrationist policies without in any way obliging the others to accept a time limit on their abstention or discrimination against them. This is recognition that diversities and differences between the nation states of Europe must be accepted, not crushed and disciplined by the imposition of a single set of laws, policies and institutions covering the whole of their affairs. There is a particular advantage in enabling the Eastern applicants to avoid participating in the common defence policy that is on the stocks. They were formerly satellites of the USSR and a number of them have a common frontier with present-day Russia. Were they all to be brought into the EU's military alliance it is not difficult to envisage that for Russia, given her history, this would be an unacceptable development.

There should be an urgent debate on a two-tier Europe and Britain should take the lead in introducing it. There is a strong pull from the majority of the British electorate for some degree of separation. It is their knowledge of this mood in the country that obliges British Ministers to act in a kind of charade in which they obstruct proposals in the European Council so that they can return home to boast of their resistance, while constantly asserting their ambition to be at the heart of Europe.

How different it will be when an open and honest British leadership, with the backing of its Parliament and people, states:

'We can go no further. But we are your friends and most reliable ally and we wish you well in your further endeavours to deepen your integration and to create whatever form of state structure that best meets your requirements and the wishes of your people'.

'We would expect no less happy and fruitful a relationship between our 58 million people and the 275 million people who have joined your political family, than now exists between the 25 million people of Canada and their great 250 million neighbour, the United States of America to the south'.

8

European Manifesto for
a Charter of Sovereignties

Adopted at an international conference organized at Nice in December 2000 by the Alliance pour la Souveraineté de la France with the support of the UK Anti-Maastricht Alliance.

In every country of Europe there is growing criticism of the functioning of the European institutions. Everywhere there are doubts about the effects of the construction of the Community. Whether the European ideal is itself well-founded has become a matter for debate.

A variety of calls for radical re-examination and of proposals for constitutional change have been put forward to resolve this crisis of confidence. They have succeeded only in increasing the confusion of public opinion, which grows steadily more disenchanted. The prospect of accelerated institutional integration and the idea of a 'hard core' or a 'pioneer group', far from opening up fruitful paths has led to fractious debate and distrust, with governments increasingly at odds with each other.

It appears that in practice the European institutions are day by day less under the control of the member States and that in parallel national governments and Parliaments, local communities, firms and individual citizens are subjected to the callous and pettifogging tutelage of the Brussels institutions. All this despite the principle of subsidiarity promulgated in the Treaties.

It is time to put an end to this uncertain drifting, to set out a clear vision for the future so as to reassure the peoples of Europe and put the construction of Europe on sound and healthy foundations.

This is why we require our governments to adopt a Charter of Sovereignties.

The Charter of Sovereignties

This Charter, whose provisions must be superior to all those of the Treaties in force, must remind us that the European Union is a free association of sovereign nations and must therefore establish:

that the member States delegate competences to the European institutions only on the basis that they are revocable, subsidiary and subordinate, and that they exclude the definition and guarantee of fundamental rights, including those of citizenship and the right to vote, which are incapable of being delegated;

that it falls ultimately to the member-States alone to control the exercise of such delegated powers, with the European Commission and Parliament being essentially subordinate and national constitutions overriding Treaty-based law in the case of any conflict between them;

that the member-States retain inalienable sovereignty in linguistic and cultural matters, particularly the right to the use of their national language on their own territory, disregarding any budgetary consideration or argument based on free competition;

that every member-State has the right to suspend any regulation in force within the European Union if it judges that necessary for the defence of its essential interests, even without the express inclusion of that right in the Treaties;

that every member-State has the right to refuse to associate itself with a decision that it deems contrary to its essential interests, with the Luxembourg Compromise requiring to be solemnly reaffirmed and majority voting, however qualified, remaining the exception;

that every member-State has the inalienable right to repatriate onto its territory competences which it has delegated to the European Union, up to and including the right to withdraw.

We are convinced that such a Charter offers the only prospect of bringing the peoples of the countries of Europe to go along with the idea of Europe by guaranteeing the genuine application of the principle of subsidiarity through the parallel application of the principle of sovereignty.

We have no doubt that a broad consensus between the governments of the countries of the European Union could be established on these principles, which put everybody on an equal footing and thereby kill off the prickly debate about their respective weight in Community decision-making.

Finally we regard it as desirable to associate immediately with us in the negotiation and signature of this Charter the applicant countries.

In this way our continent will once more be able to contemplate its future with ambition, optimism and composure.

9

Limits to EU Integration

Lord Owen

In 1789 the fledgling Constitution of the United States was amended by the addition of a bill of rights in twelve Amendments. By 2004 it might be possible to amend the European Convention on Human Rights to incorporate some of the new provisions proposed in the EU's Charter of Fundamental Rights. That Charter has not and will not have by then the maturity and acceptability of the European Convention which has won acceptance in the wider Europe and is one of the few structures to bind in almost all those who can reasonably look to eventual EU membership.

The First Amendment

The European Union is not a country and shall not create from its Member States a single state. It is a unique Union, part supranational, part inter-governmental. Its parliamentarians must be elected by the Member States and should reflect these divided responsibilities in that accountability for the supranational institutions should lie with the European Parliament and that for the inter-governmental part of the Union with the National Parliaments of the Member States.

The Second Amendment

The Union shall levy no taxes. Member states have the right to retain the power to conduct their own economic policy which would include amongst others monetary, taxation and social benefit policies. No national law regulating the taxation of income or profits shall be construed as an obstacle to the free movement of goods, or services or capital.

The Third Amendment

Member States have the right, following the procedures in the Treaties, to retain the ultimate power of independent action over foreign and defence policy within the framework of Common Foreign and Security Policy and European Defence and Security Policy.

The Fourth Amendment

Member States are not bound to give legal force to decisions of the European Court of Justice unless those legal powers directly stem from Treaties ratified under the procedures of the Union.

The Fifth Amendment

The Union and Member States shall uphold the principle of subsidiarity and the responsibility for determining what powers from the inception of the Treaties should be returned to Member States should be that of the European Council taking into account the views of the European Commission and the European Parliament.

The Sixth Amendment

The Union and its Member States shall respect the fundamental rights of its citizens, including, but not limited to, those rights guaranteed by the European Convention for the Protection of Human Rights and Fundamental Freedoms, signed in Rome on 4th November 1950, and rights common among Member States.

The Seventh Amendment

Member States may leave the Union at any time, after a period of no less than six months of consultation with other Member States and the European Commission, reflecting the reality that the commitment to an ever closer union is of its peoples and not the Member States of the EU.

The Eighth Amendment

The European Council, one for each Member State, shall be the high policy making body of the Union. The President of the Council shall be drawn from its members on an agreed rotation and there shall be no direct elections across the Union for a President of the EU nor for the President of the Commission. The European Council shall give instructions and guidance to the Council of Ministers and to the European Commission which shall normally be published after each meeting along with voting records. An Agenda shall be published before all Council of Ministers meetings. A voting record shall be published immediately afterwards.

These eight Amendments could only be changed in part or whole by a ratification procedure involving the unanimous approval of all Member States.

10

SOS Democracy's thirteen Demands

1. The Nice Treaty draft must be renegotiated since it weakens parliamentary democracy in our countries. This should be part of the process leading to a new treaty in 2004.

2. The future fundamental treaty must not be a constitution for a European federation but an international treaty respecting the parliamentary democracies and the national sovereignty of the member states, including a recognised right to leave the European Union, with clear rules for its exercise.

3. The treaty must include a catalogue of competences and explicitly state that the competence to legislate resides in national parliaments unless the treaty gives this right, in a specified and clearly defined area, to the European institutions.

4. The competences at EU-level must be limited to trade and common minimum rules for the protection of the environment and consumers, together with such concrete measures as cannot be solved at nation state level because of the international nature of the problem or the demonstrable extra value added through co-operation. It is for national parliaments to decide if they want to move a decision to a higher level.

5. The supranational institutions must never again be able to

develop their own competences through the Commission's monopoly over decision-making processes and the frequently revolutionary judgments of the Court of Justice in Luxembourg. Instead community initiatives should be left to a council comprising e.g. 20 representatives from each national parliament. They could meet twice a year and adopt the rolling program for legislation, including the legal bases, and propose changes in the catalogue of competences. Decisions and recommendations could be made by qualified majority, with reasonably negotiated opt-outs for those countries not willing to participate in the areas chosen for common legislation.

6. When the initiative is returned to elected representatives, the European Commission should be made accountable to the Council of Ministers and prepare balanced proposals in co-operation with the member states. The Commission must always be composed of one representative from each national parliament, and each Commissioner must attend a meeting of a European control committee in a national parliament once weekly.

7. Negotiations over legislation must take place in public meetings of the Council of Ministers, the European Parliament and national parliaments. The Council must comprise one minister from each country and each should have only one vote. The European Parliament could continue with the existing format for distribution of seats. For a law to come into force it must be passed with majorities in both the Council and the Parliament and also in national parliaments. If a national parliament is not willing to adopt a piece of common legislation a flexible solution can be found in a balanced opt-out, which ensures it is seen to that the opt-out does not harm the majority of member states whilst the state in question can keep its freedom of choice.

8. The existing legislation, comprising more than 20,000 regulations, directives and other legally binding decisions, must be examined in order to:

a) Return to the member states all legislation that cannot be proven to be of a nature to justify cross-border law.

b) Introduce more freedom in legislation, minimise its use and encourage mutual recognition instead of total harmonisation; careful co-ordination and framework agreements instead of too many detailed regulations etc.

c) Introduce a sunset clause in most pieces of legislation, making them automatically obsolete, unless they are confirmed after a reasonable period of time.

d) Introduce more flexibility so that all laws do not necessarily encompass and bind all citizens and countries. For instance detailed regulations on the size of strawberries should be binding only on trans-border trade between grocers without being applied at local markets and supermarkets.

e) All new legislative proposals must be subjected to a full Regulatory Impact Assessment (RIA) conducted at least in accordance with OECD protocols and no such proposal may proceed unless benefits demonstrably outweigh costs.

9. The EU Charter of Fundamental Rights must be clarified and amended to include these three important provisos:

a) If there is a conflict in the interpretation of the European Convention of Human Rights between the European Court of Human Rights in Strasbourg and the Court of Justice in Luxembourg, the pan-European interpretation must be binding on the EU.

b) If there is a conflict in the interpretation of human rights and ground rules in the national constitutions or bills of rights *vis-a-vis* the EU Charter, the EU authorities must accept the interpretation of national high courts or constitutional courts.

c) The Charter must bind only the European institutions and those member states that decide to be bound by it.

10. The European institutions must adopt a modern administrative code as proposed by the European Ombudsman, which includes clear rules for openness. This includes a right of access to all documents unless a qualified majority has made a reasoned exemption. This exemption can be brought to appeal before the European Ombudsman who would have the authority to support a justified claim.

11. All national representatives in the EU decision-making process must be accountable to, paid by and taxed by their national authorities to avoid the establishment of a special European elite disdainful of electorates.

12. All accepted democratic applicant countries must be offered full participation in the European decision making process. They must be offered flexible membership conditions including permanent derogations and long-term transition measures and adequate help to overcome their economic and environmental shortcomings.

13. Future treaties must be submitted to legally binding referenda in all countries where the national constitution permits it.

[Editor's Note: SOS Democracy is an official intergroup in the European Parliament. Its Chairman is Jens-Peter Bonde, its Secretary is Daniel Hannan]

11

The Manifesto of Czech Eurorealism of the ODS (Civic Democratic Party)

Jan Zahradil, Petr Plecit, Petr Adrian and Miloslav Bednax

The accession of the Czech Republic to the EU is not politically neutral. As the most extensive voluntary transfer of part of our sovereignty to a supranational level it is a profoundly political act. We have to realise on what conditions we are to join the EU and decide which model of the Union we shall support as a fully-fledged member.

The present situation and future trends of the EU

The process of integration involves a number of aspects which overlap and may conflict. One of them is the confrontation of European interests (those of European bureaucracy, European institutions and Member States) with the interests of other world centres. Another is the clash of interests between the European bureaucracy and the Member States, while a third is confrontation between regional and other interests within each Member State and within the EU as a whole.

The European states are characterized by costly bureaucratic redistributive processes which tend to reduce global competitiveness and stifle economic development. The single market is bound by tens of thousands of pages of regulation whose purpose is to serve as a protectionist instrument sheltering the European market.

The European institutions suffer from a 'democratic deficit' and have little respect and authority among the public. This results from their lack of transparency and controllability as well as by the fact that few citizens of Member States identify themselves with the concept of European citizenship.

The ambition of European states to assume greater responsibility for their own security holds within it an implicit anti-Americanism and a desire for world power status, but disregards the fact that the efficiency of European armed forces is several times lower than that of the US and that there is absolutely no prospect of their defence expenditure being raised by one-third to American levels. If the Common Foreign and Security Policy of the EU were to lead to a separation of Europe from the US and the creation of structures parallel to or even competitive with NATO the vital interest of European democratic civilisation would be undermined.

There are two models for the future direction of the EU, the inter-governmental or the supranational. The former consists of multilateral co-operation on equal terms, the latter a unified European state. In practice the EU has always displayed a combination of the two. The supranational political union was presented as the most progressive, with the European Parliament to be developed as a genuine legislative body and the European Commission taking on the role of the European government. The most prominent symbol of this approach is the political project of Economic and Monetary Union, to be followed by the unification of tax and social systems. The drive in this federalist direction has been slowed in recent years, partly because of lessening French support, and the change may be seen in the failure of the Treaty of Nice to make the advances that might have been expected on the transfer of fresh competences to the Union, the binding inclusion of the Charter of Fundamental Human Rights and major extension of qualified majority voting.

However, the federalists, particularly Germany, have revived the multi-speed concept in the form of a 'hard-core' of integrationist states who would thereby avoid being slowed down by the rest. A vigorous struggle may be expected in 2004 at the next Inter-Governmental Conference.

The Project of Enlargement to the East

This project is not aimed at the speediest possible accession of the applicant countries but, rather, at the exploitation of the pre-accession process for the benefit of the existing members. The candidate countries are seen above all as markets for EU products and as a source of raw materials and cheap labour. At present economic exchange between the EU and individual candidate countries is asymmetric, operating to the benefit of the Union, while the process generates jobs within the EU and thus supports part of its social subsystem. Even without tariffs the EU has effective protection mechanisms, whereas the candidates were obliged in their association agreements to open up their markets to an extraordinary extent. For the EU a country is much more attractive as a candidate than a fully-fledged member. Rapid enlargement is incompatible with many other interests of existing members, such as their share of financial assistance, their higher wage levels and the benefits they derive from the Common Agricultural Policy. Popular support for enlargement has fallen steeply within the EU.

EU negotiators have skilfully managed the process of enlargement as a competition between the applicants and prevented them from adopting a common approach. They demanded an unconditional acceptance of the *acquis communautaire*, which is essentially an anti-dumping measure that will do away with the competitive advantages hitherto enjoyed by the applicants, such as lower labour and production costs. The pressure to integrate Community law has been imposed far more stringently than ever before, at a time when its volume far exceeded what existed in earlier enlargements. Successful implementation of the *acquis* is judged solely by European officials, which enables them to determine at any time the relative placing of each candidate.

Enlargement depends strictly on political will within the Union, which is shown by the fact that some applicants could already have been admitted. But applicant countries made a serious mistake at the beginning when they focused on the quantitative aspect (membership as soon as possible) instead of the qualitative aspect (conditions of membership). They should have been asking what sort of EU they wished to be in and now they find the EU determined to suspend for a long period of time at least two of its own fundamental freedoms, the free movement of people and goods. Financial assistance from EU funds will be limited for the applicants, certainly lower than that currently provided. Enlargement may provide only a limited, second-rate membership for some time.

The Czech Republic and the EU

Czech statehood depends on a permanently inspiring formulation of national identity and state sovereignty. It has always tended to the liberal democratic form of government and a freely established democratic European unity of loosely connected and co-operating states would be perfectly compatible with it. Whereas present-day European social democracy with its central redistributive processes and the politically centrist Catholicism of Christian democracy are contrary to the founding ideals of the Czech state.

We have to monitor further developments in the light of Czech national interests, i.e. territorial integrity, political sovereignty and the mutual opening and integration of markets. What we want is the inter-governmental model and a form of European integration that proceeds upwards from the bottom, from European nations and their citizens, represented by their parliaments and their governments. It must not come from the offices of a European elite.

We have had historical experience of a non-homogeneous federative entity which leads us to reject imposed federation. The theory of the inevitable decline of the nation-state and its replacement by a supranational federation contradicts European democratic history for it disregards such fundamental prerequisites of a stable state as common language and political culture. This theory reduces national identity to a merely folkloristic culture and fails to take into account its political and constitutional significance, based on the political concept of a nation as the source of state sovereignty and constitutional legitimacy.

Similarly the idea that nation-states are going to be swept away by regionalisation must be rejected. Many of the existing regional movements are provincial and anti-modernist rather than anti-centrist, seeking to shelter their region from the world.

At the same time time the argument that small states need the protection of supranationality is equally erroneous. It is the broadest possible inter-governmental approach that provides a defence against dictatorial behaviour by great powers, for each state can exercise a national veto. This means that the

European Council is the most legitimate organ of the EU because it consists of national representatives.

The answer to the question of what form of EU we should support must include the rejection of any further transfer of competences to the European Commission or Parliament. There is no European public and no European electorate, so that the EP can never become a genuine parliamentary institution reflecting all-European interests. We must oppose any further limitation of national vetoes or extension of qualified majority voting, together with the inclusion of the Charter of Fundamental Human Rights in the treaties and the adoption of a constitution. In an enlarged EU only a multi-speed model would be viable and its foundations already exist. Some states must be able to opt out of common policies without preventing the participation of others, so that there is a menu from which some states can select areas for closer integration. But the interpretation of flexibility as providing for a vanguard leads to inequality in the status of individual states and must be rejected.

Economic and Monetary Union is primarily a political project whose economics are doubtful and our entry to it would have to follow a referendum. Certainly we must reject the potential fiscal union, which is another step to a federal state and would also serve the interests of countries with extensive social systems by depriving others of competitive advantage.

The basis of our negotiations on accession must be full and undeferred participation in the Union's decision-making processes and in the single market. We should insist on participating fully in the decisions about the future of the EU at the Inter-Governmental Conference in 2004, wherever we stand in the accession process. We have been in integrated complexes before all of which eventually disintegrated and it would be a mistake to see the contemporary EU as an indisputable finality.

Alternative, Substitute and other Solutions

The EU could postpone accession if we defend Czech interests vigorously but it could not adequately compensate us for a long-term exclusion from the fundamental freedoms of the single market. Alternatives have therefore to be contemplated, particularly if there are attempts to dismantle the transatlantic security link and NATO. Membership of the European Free Trade Association (EFTA) or the European Economic Area (EEA) would give access to the single market while leaving the Republic free to negotiate trade links with other countries and groupings. This course would partially reduce the huge burden of EU social, labour environmental and consumer legislation. Another possibility would be to negotiate a bilateral arrangement with the EU as Switzerland has done.

As a member of EFTA and EEA the Republic could seek to establish a connexion with NAFTA, particularly now that the importance of geographic distance is diminishing in global trade. Our vision must be that of a broad Euro-Atlantic area with economic, political and security links, not a fortress Europe.

[Editor's Note: Available in a fuller version on www.euobserv-er.com and in the European Journal 9/1 September 2001]

12

For a Europe of Democracies - Against the Europe of Nations

Paul Ruppen

Co-operation and local liberty of political action

International relations are becoming more and more important. This is a positive development for those concerned with the politics of peace. What is more, international co-operation is essential to widen the range of political action and the ability of states to solve their problems democratically. Without such co-operation the struggle for national competitive advantage will overwhelm the desire to solve social and environmental problems. On the other hand, international co-operation alone cannot assist states in their search for solutions.

The European Union and the GATT/WTO demonstrate that international co-operation may impose competition on countries and regions and lead thereby to social and environmental dumping. There is, therefore, an urgent need to develop forms of international co-operation that preserve its advantages while avoiding the disadvantages inherent in co-operation of the EU pattern. The aims of such an alternative development must be a decentralised, co-operative global society, the strengthening of local, regional, 'national' and transnational democracy and the avoidance of euronational bloc-building. A model will be developed here of international co-operation that respects local, democratic self-determination (subject always to the protection of human rights of all people in the area).

Transnational democracy

a) Existing states need to be decentralised and democratised. Decentralisation should be brought about by assigning competences to the lowest possible level within a state. Democratisation should be brought about by the introduction of direct democracy at every level of the state (communities, areas, districts, regions, cantons etc.). Every local political authority should have the right to conclude international treaties - within its range of competences - with every foreign political entity.

b) International relations also have to be decentralised and democratised.

Decentralisation is achieved by solving problems at the lowest posssible political level. Only those problems which cannot be solved independently should be solved by international co-operation and then only by the countries directly concerned. The traffic problems of the Alps have to be solved by the Alpine regions. The problems of North Sea fisheries, which do not concern the Alpine regions, should be solved only by the North Sea coastal countries. The application of principles developed in this way would result in a fine and dense network of co-operation without the creation of blocs.

Democratisation of international relations needs to be introduced by greater involvement of the populations of the various states in international negotiations. To achieve this we propose the following reforms:

1. Principle of free access to information. Political authorities are duty-bound to inform the population about current and planned international negotiations; all official negotiating documents have to be published;

2. Institution of conferences at which different social interests can be articulated (e.g. extra-parliamentary commissions where non-governmental organisations (NGOs) are represented);

3. Right of citizens of the different countries to put forward proposals at the international level (OSCE, UNO, EU, WEU, NATO, environmental conferences etc.).

4. Constitutional obligation on governments to support people's right to participate at the national and international levels.

c) Minimal social and environmental standards (minimal norms with regard to working hours, social charges, environmental taxes etc.) are to be introduced to prevent social and environmental dumping. These standards may be subject to improvement in particular countries or groups of countries provided this does not damage poorer countries and can be expected to improve in any case in the course of events. This model permits different countries to experiment with different solutions to problems, a potentially beneficial procedure for all. NGOs (such as trade unions, peace movement, women's movement, environmental movements, consumer protection movements and peasant movements) play an important part in this context. They provide a counterweight to the power of private corporation lobbies, which are themselves NGOs of a special kind. The 'divide and rule' strategy of international capital can be countered by the intensive exchange of information and making it available to the public. NGOs should therefore have the right to participate in international conferences and have their delegates included in international discussions.

d) An international clearing house should be developed within which countries' financial surpluses and deficits would be balanced and which would at the same time make it easier to help poorer countries. Such a system would stabilise exchange rates by fixing them to units based on the real values of goods and reduce constraints on countries' ability to pursue independent economic policies. Existing proposals for such a reorganisation of the monetary system offer a realistic prospect for different countries to pursue flexible economic policies that are adapted to their own situations and promote full employment in line with national labour practices (e.g. Paul Davidson *Economics for a Civilized Society*, Macmillan 1988). The common aim of these measures against social and environmental dumping and for international monetary reform depend on international co-operation in order to permit greater freedom of decision-making at the local level. Some kinds of co-operation lead to more local freedom, while some (EU, GATT/WTO) to less. We oppose those forms of international co-operation which place unnecessary limits on local problem-solving.

The advantages of direct democracy

Direct democracy is the political system that permits a statutorily defined percentage of the electorate to require a vote on an issue. It permits the people to assign competences to different levels of the political structure. Direct democracy, which is realised in an imperfect way in several States of the USA and in Switzerland, maximises political participation by the people. Participation of this sort should be treated as a human right extending to every man and woman, including foreigners, permitting them to share in building the social, economic and political framework in which they have to live. The value of direct democracy is not to be argued on the basis that the people can be trusted. Blind confidence in the people as a whole - or in elites - is dangerous. It is not the political system that guarantees a man the defence of his values and ideas but his own actions. Direct democracy offers an ideal framework for them because relatively small groups can demand political discussion of an issue. Nowadays political understanding is more widespread among the population.

To accept the advantages of direct democracy does not require us to deny that the results of votes reflect the realities of the distribution of social and economic power. To advocate a system does not mean that we should attribute any mystique to it. All political systems reflect power relations so that this point should not be urged against direct democracy alone. Under direct democracy reforms can be made that promote opportunities for weaker groups to influence political decisions in their favour. But one cannot demand from it that it always produces 'correct' decisions. No political procedures can ensure the 'correctness' of decisions. All of them suffer from a lack of respect for minorities but direct democracy offers a framework at least as good as any other for action to redress this and to promote human rights. The recent recognition of women's rights to participate in elections and other votes in Switzerland is not an argument against direct democracy. Before the introduction of political rights for women the Swiss system suffered from a lack of direct democracy insofar as it excluded a majority of citizens from participation. Similarly, the exclusion of foreigners is a restriction of direct democracy and actually amounts to an argument for extending it and bringing about the full political integration of all foreigners.

Once there is in place a system of direct democracy it is the people, not parliaments, that lose their power to a centralisation process such as integration in the EU. Parliaments do not necessarily defend their power as individual MPs pursue their personal careers and sacrifice the power of their institution in favour of their personal aims. The safest bulwark against EU-type European integration is direct democracy in the hands of people.

[Editor's Note: Statement for the Forum for Direct Democracy, www.europa-magazin.ch]

13

A Better Europe: Forward from the Treaty of London

Lionel Bell

Laeken and the European Constitution

The Treaty signed at Nice was not merely another in the series that has given the central institutions of the European Union more and more of the governmental powers that previously belonged to the member states and, through them, to their peoples. Declaration 23 of the Inter-Governmental Conference required the Swedish and Belgian Presidencies during the year 2001 to prepare for another Conference in 2004 which is intended to mark the emergence of the Union into full statehood. Its powers and procedures will be enshrined in a Constitution, of which the Charter of Fundamental Rights will form a predestined part, and which will be capable of overriding the constitutional protection provided at national level to the peoples of Europe. Para. 5 of the Declaration reads as follows:

The process should address *inter alia* the following questions:

how to establish and monitor a more precise delimitation of powers between the European Union and the Member States, reflecting the principle of subsidiarity;

the status of the Charter of Fundamental Rights of the European Union, proclaimed in Nice, in accordance with the conclusions of the European Council in Cologne;

A. a simplification of the Treaties with a view to making them clearer and better understood without changing their meaning;

B. the role of national Parliaments in the European architecture.

The requirement to ratify the Nice Treaty and the subsequent confirmation at Laeken in December 2001 of the decision to hold a Constitutional Convention for the Union offer an opportunity to halt the centralising process; only thereafter can it be reversed in favour of the nations. It is acknowledged in all quarters that what is missing from the European Union is democracy. Its institutions combine to form a government that generates legislation behind closed doors, that cannot be called to account, that is not required to submit itself to the people so that it might be dismissed. This is not a democratic deficit, it is a democratic void and it is inevitable in an organization that evidently intends to exercise virtually all the powers of government across the territory of the existing Union and, if possible, throughout Europe. For there is not a European people capable of conducting a coherent political discourse on the basis of which a government might be put into place with the credentials and authority of contested election. What we get instead is pettifogging bureaucratic administration subject to processes of lobbying, haggling and blackmail. It has been cruelly observed that if the European Union applied for membership of itself it would be rejected for having inadequate democratic credentials.

Only national democracy has the ability to reconcile individual interests within a larger society by making it possible for those interests to exercise influence from the bottom up. Experience shows that the representative institutions that do this cannot work properly unless their governments exercise the sovereignty that belongs to the nation, not to powerful individuals. This sovereignty is inseparable from national democracy, a point which has to be accepted as fundamental before we can go on to examine how to secure the benefits of international co-operation. A level of democracy, of government, of sovereignty superior to the national level cannot succeed unless and until there is a genuine people in existence at the higher level. Such a people cannot be manufactured into existence by inventing in advance the governmental institutions that they might work out for themselves over centuries.

A sovereign nation is the sole authority for making legislative and other governmental decisions to be implemented within its territory but may choose to limit the operation of its sovereignty in specific respects by agreement with other nations. Such a choice is reversible, though that is not a step to be taken lightly.

To support international co-operation and agreements it is valuable to have some institutional framework to ensure full and fair implementation. Evasion is always likely to be suspected and suspicions are all too often justified. At the same time, beyond defined areas in which agreements may be worked out conflicts of interest between countries will continue to arise and their handling may benefit from the existence of an institution in which differences can be explored and heat replaced by light. To recognise this is not to depreciate the role of conventional bilateral and multilateral diplomacy nor to deny the value of the United Nations in enabling countries to get along with each other. But there is also a place for regional arrangements, particularly in Europe, where competitition between countries is widely believed to have been responsible for the continent's pre-eminent place in the world as well as its record of conflict.

But the development of the European Union on its path of intrusive homogenization enforced by supra-government, supra-legislation and supra-judiciary does not meet the requirement. The framework that could do so already exists.

The Treaty of London and the original Council of Europe

In the aftermath of the most destructive conflict that the world has ever seen, not least in Europe, the evident need to bring the nations of Europe together led to the Congress of Europe in the Hague on 7th May 1948, which was followed on 5th May 1949 by the signature in St James's Palace, London of the Treaty establishing the Council of Europe. Extracts from the Statute of the Council are annexed. 40 European countries now belong to the Council and their governments could usefully pay it a great deal more attention than they do. Like the United Nations the Council was established on the basis of sovereign nations co-operating for their mutual benefit, but there were those for whom this basis was insufficient. They wished for much closer integration and in this mood established in 1951 the Iron and Steel Community as a firmly supra-national body, the original element of what is now the Union.

The Parliamentary Assembly, which later became the Parliament of the eventual European Union, was first accommodated in Council buildings in Strasbourg. During its development the Union has also taken over both the flag and the anthem of the Council and much of its nomenclature. It would not be too much to say that it has virtually displaced its predecessor in the public mind. The time has surely come for more extensive use to be made of the Council, with its greater inclusiveness and the absence of supranational ambitions, to enable the nations of Europe to work together for their common good. While the inter-governmental nature of the Council provides no guarantee that its activities or those of its elements will always display good sense it must be remembered that they are in the hands of governments who are themselves accountable and can exercise direction. Among the greatest drawbacks of the Union is the near impossibility of getting a decision reversed.

A development of the Council of Europe

If two or more governments of European countries, working within the context of their own constitutional arrangements, decide for their mutual benefit to enter into an agreement covering some defined topic, that agreement might be deposited with the Council. The agreement could provide that any individual resident within a country that is party to the agreement or any enterprise established within such a country or the government of such a country, upon considering themselves damaged by evasion of the agreement in another country could require an arbitration. This procedure might extend to cases in which the government of a country causes external damage by failing to implement its own legislation as well as international agreements in a proper and reasonable manner. Each country concerned would appoint one appropriate expert to the arbitration panel, who might be supported, if necessary, by a team. The Council itself would similarly appoint an appropriate expert to serve as chairman of the panel.

A panel finding in favour of a complainant could order such

redress and reform as it found appropriate. Failure to comply with such an order in respect of an agreement to which this procedure had been made applicable would constitute a substantial breach capable of leading to its termination.

The potential application of the procedure does not end there. Working groups could be established in the same way as arbitration panels in order to elaborate parts of existing agreements or even to support the preparation of domestic legislation. Countries could legislate to make the findings of panels or some of them directly enforceable in their courts.

UN Economic Commission for Europe

In matters of trade, which form a large part of the co-operation between countries, this procedure could be supported by the involvement of the United Nations Economic Commission for Europe (UN/ECE). This body was set up in 1947 by the UN Economic and Social Council. It is a forum where 55 countries of North America, Western, Central and Eastern Europe and Central Asia come together to forge the tools of their economic co-operation without giving up their right to take independent decisions. All interested UN member states have observer status and may participate in its work. Over 70 international professional organizations and other non-governmental organizations which have consultative status with the Economic and Social Council, take part in UN/ECE activities.

Co-operation, information sharing and joint action take place across a wide range of activities. The main areas of activity of UN/ECE are economic analysis, environment and human settlements, statistics, sustainable energy, trade, industry and enterprise development, timber and transport.

UN/ECE has drawn up more than thirty conventions and protocols, and over 250 regulations and standards. These instruments eliminate obstacles and simplify procedures throughout the region and with the rest of the world. A number of them also aim at improving the environment. UN/ECE in this way provides consumer guarantees of safety and quality, helps to protect the environment, and facilitates trade. It also strengthens the integration of member states at the regional and international level.

Conclusion

It should not be supposed that this proposal for a Better Europe is put forward in the belief that the principles can be elaborated with ease or that the negotiation of agreements will continue to be anything but painfully difficult. All that is asserted is that the proposal is capable of being put into practice and that by abandoning the ambition to create a single country, a Great Power, it offers Europeans the prospect of living together in a genuine harmony as opposed to the fractious fiasco that the European Union is becoming.

The initial requirement is for the government of a country to give notice that it intends no longer to be bound by the European Union Treaties or some part of them - a declaration to which there is no bar under international law - or is withdrawing its application for membership of the European Union - and stands ready to enter into agreements with other countries in the manner described. A difficult period of negotiation may be expected to follow but it would not be practicable to explore it at this stage.

The procedure is applicable to agreements in a wide range of areas, including trade, immigration and border controls, crime, public health and environmental pollution. It is not difficult to see that mutual benefit can be brought about in these matters nor that there is the possibility of profiting from evasion.

The following extracts from the founding documents of the Council of Europe and the UN Economic Commission demonstrate that they reflect ideals shared by many genuine supporters of European co-operation who have become increasingly disturbed and disappointed by the authoritarian direction taken by the EU.

[Editor's Note: Further information on these organizations is available at websites www.coe.int and www.unece.org respectively]

Annex I

Statute of the Council of Europe - London 5.V.1949 (extracts)

Preamble
Chapter I - Aim of the Council of Europe
Chapter II - Membership
Chapter III - General
Chapter X - Final provisions

Preamble

The Governments of the Kingdom of Belgium, the Kingdom of Denmark, the French Republic, the Irish Republic, the Italian Republic, the Grand Duchy of Luxembourg, the Kingdom of the Netherlands, the Kingdom of Norway, the Kingdom of Sweden and the United Kingdom of Great Britain and Northern Ireland;

Convinced that the pursuit of peace based upon justice and international co-operation is vital for the preservation of human society and civilisation;

Reaffirming their devotion to the spiritual and moral values which are the common heritage of their peoples and the true source of individual freedom, political liberty and the rule of law, principles which form the basis of all genuine democracy;

Believing that, for the maintenance and further realisation of these ideals and in the interests of economic and social progress, there is a need of a closer unity between all like-minded countries of Europe;

Considering that, to respond to this need and to the expressed aspirations of their peoples in this regard, it is necessary forthwith to create an organisation which will bring European States into closer association;

Have in consequence decided to set up a Council of Europe consisting of a committee of representatives of governments and of a consultative assembly, and have for this purpose adopted the following Statute.

Chapter I - Aim of the Council of Europe

Article 1

A. The aim of the Council of Europe is to achieve a greater unity between its members for the purpose of safeguarding and realising the ideals and principles which are their common heritage and facilitating their economic and social progress.

B. This aim shall be pursued through the organs of the Council by discussion of questions of common concern and by agreements and common action in economic, social, cultural, scientific, legal and administrative matters and in the maintenance and further realisation of human rights and fundamental freedoms.

C. Participation in the Council of Europe shall not affect the collaboration of its members in the work of the United Nations and of other international organisations or unions to which they are parties.

D. Matters relating to national defence do not fall within the scope of the Council of Europe.

Chapter II - Membership

Article 2

The members of the Council of Europe are the Parties to this Statute.

Article 3

Every member of the Council of Europe must accept the principles of the rule of law and of the enjoyment by all persons within its jurisdiction of human rights and fundamental freedoms, and collaborate sincerely and effectively in the realisation of the aim of the Council as specified in Chapter *1*.

Article 4

Any European State which is deemed to be able and willing to fulfil the provisions of Article 3 may be invited to become a member of the Council of Europe by the Committee of Ministers. Any State so invited shall become a member on the deposit on its behalf with the Secretary General of an instrument of accession to the present Statute.

Article 5

A. In special circumstances, a European country which is deemed to be able and willing to fulfil the provisions of Article

3 may be invited by the Committee of Ministers to become an associate member of the Council of Europe. Any country so invited shall become an associate member on the deposit on its behalf with the Secretary General of an instrument accepting the present Statute. An associate member shall be entitled to be represented in the Consultative Assembly only.

B. The expression 'member' in this Statute includes an associate member except when used in connexion with representation on the Committee of Ministers.

Article 6

Before issuing invitations under Article 4 or 5 above, the Committee of Ministers shall determine the number of representatives on the Consultative Assembly to which the proposed member shall be entitled and its proportionate financial contribution.

Article 7

Any member of the Council of Europe may withdraw by formally notifying the Secretary General of its intention to do so. Such withdrawal shall take effect at the end of the financial year in which it is notified, if the notification is given during the first nine months of that financial year. If the notification is given in the last three months of the financial year, it shall take effect at the end of the next financial year.

Article 8

Any member of the Council of Europe which has seriously violated Article 3 may be suspended from its rights of representation and requested by the Committee of Ministers to withdraw under Article 7. If such member does not comply with this request, the Committee may decide that it has ceased to be a member of the Council as from such date as the Committee may determine.

Article 9

The Committee of Ministers may suspend the right of representation on the Committee and on the Consultative Assembly of a member which has failed to fulfil its financial obligation during such period as the obligation remains unfulfilled.

Chapter III - General

Article 10

The organs of the Council of Europe are:
i. the Committee of Ministers;
ii. the Consultative Assembly.

Both these organs shall be served by the Secretariat of the Council of Europe.

Article 11

The seat of the Council of Europe is at Strasbourg.

Article 12

The official languages of the Council of Europe are English and French. The rules of procedure of the Committee of Ministers and of the Consultative Assembly shall determine in what circumstances and under what conditions other languages may be used.

(The members of the Council and the number of seats they hold in the Consultative Assembly are shown below)

Albania	4	Lithuania	4
Andorra	2	Luxembourg	3
Austria	6	Malta	3
Belgium	7	Moldova	5
Bulgaria	6	Netherlands	7
Croatia	5	Norway	5
Cyprus	3	Poland	12
Czech Republic	7	Portugal	7
Denmark	5	Romania	10
Estonia	3	Russia	18
Finland	5	San Marino	2
France	18	Slovak Republic	5
Germany	18	Slovenia	3
Greece	7	Spain	12
Hungary	7	Sweden	6
Iceland	3	Switzerland	6
Ireland	4	'the former Yugoslav Republic of Macedonia'	3
Italy	18	Turkey	12
Liechtenstein	2	Ukraine	12
Latvia	3	United Kingdom of Great Britain and Northern Ireland	18

Chapter X - Final provisions

Article 42

A. This Statute shall be ratified. Ratifications shall be deposited with the Government of the United Kingdom of Great

Britain and Northern Ireland.

B. The present Statute shall come into force as soon as seven instruments of ratification have been deposited. The Government of the United Kingdom shall transmit to all signatory governments a certificate declaring that the Statute has entered into force and giving the names of the members of the Council of Europe on that date.

C. Thereafter each other signatory shall become a Party to this Statute as from the date of the deposit of its instrument of ratification.

In witness whereof the undersigned, being duly authorised thereto, have signed the present Statute.

Done at London, this 5th day of May 1949, in English and French, both texts being equally authentic, in a single copy which shall remain deposited in the archives of the Government of the United Kingdom which shall transmit certified copies to the other signatory governments.

Annex II

Terms of reference and rules of procedure of the United Nations Economic Commission for Europe (Extracts)

Terms of reference

1. The Economic Commission for Europe, acting within the framework of the policies of the United Nations and subject to the general supervision of the Council shall, provided that the Commission takes no action in respect to any country without the agreement of the Government of that country:

a) Initiate and participate in measures for facilitating concerted action for the economic reconstruction of Europe, for raising the level of European economic activity, and for maintaining and strengthening the economic relations of the European countries both among themselves and with other countries of the world;

b) Make or sponsor such investigations and studies of economic and technological problems of and developments within member countries of the Commission and within Europe generally as the Commission deems appropriate;

c) Undertake or sponsor the collection, evaluation and dissemination of such economic, technological and statistical information as the Commission deems appropriate.

7. The members of the Commission are the European Members of the United Nations, the United States of America, Canada, Switzerland and Israel. Insofar as the former USSR was a European Member of the United Nations, new members of the United Nations that had been constituent republics located in the Asian part of the former USSR are entitled to be members of the UN/ECE.

11. The Commission shall invite any Member of the United Nations not a member of the Commission to participate in a consultative capacity in its consideration of any matter of particular concern to that non-member.

12. The Commission shall invite representatives of specialized agencies and may invite representatives of any inter-governmental organizations to participate in a consultative capacity in its consideration of any matter of particular concern to that agency or organization, following the practices of the Economic and Social Council.

13. The Commission shall make arrangements for consultation with non-governmental organizations which have been granted consultative status by the Economic and Social Council, in accordance with the principles approved by the Council for this purpose and contained in Council resolution 1296 (XLIV) parts I and II.

18. The headquarters of the Commission shall be located at the seat of the European Office of the United Nations.

Rules of procedure of the commission

Chapter III

Representation and credentials

Rule 9
Each member shall be represented on the Commission by an accredited representative.

Rule 10
A representative may be accompanied to the sessions of the Commission by alternate representatives and advisers and, when absent, he may be replaced by an alternate representative.

Rule 11
The credentials of each representative appointed to the Commission, together with a designation of alternate representatives, shall be submitted to the Executive Secretary without delay.

Rule 12
The Chairperson and the Vice-Chairpersons shall examine the credentials and report upon them to the Commission.

Chapter VII

Voting

Rule 34
Each member of the Commission shall have one vote.

Rule 35
Decisions of the Commission shall be made by a majority of the members present and voting.

Rule 36
The Commission shall take no action in respect of any country without the agreement of the Government of that country.

Rule 37
The Commission shall normally vote by show of hands. If any representative requests a roll call, a roll call shall be taken in the English alphabetical order of the names of the members.

Rule 38
All elections shall be decided by secret ballot, unless, in the absence of any objection, the Commission decides to proceed without taking a ballot on an agreed candidate or state.

Rule 39
If a vote is equally divided upon matters other than elections, a second vote shall be taken at the next meeting. If this vote also results in equality, the proposal shall be regarded as rejected.

Chapter X

Publicity of meetings

Rule 46
The meetings of the Commission shall ordinarily be held in public. The Commission may decide that a particular meeting

or meetings shall be held in private.

The June Press

www.junepress.com

Europe of Many Circles:
Constructing a Wider Europe
by Richard Body
New European Publications. Price £14.95

The Breakdown of Europe
by Richard Body
New European Publications. Price £9.95

Associated, Not Absorbed.
The Associated European Area: a constructive
alternative to a single European state
by Bill Cash MP
European Foundation. Price £6.00

Separate Ways
by Peter Shore
Duckworth. Price £18.99

Limits to EU Integration
by Lord Owen
Centre for Policy Studies. Price £5.00

These books and more are available by post from:

The June Press
PO Box 119
Totnes, Devon TQ9 7WA

Tel: 01548-821402
Fax: 01548-821574
E-mail: info@junepress.com

Please add P+P - 10% UK, 20% Europe, 30% Rest of World